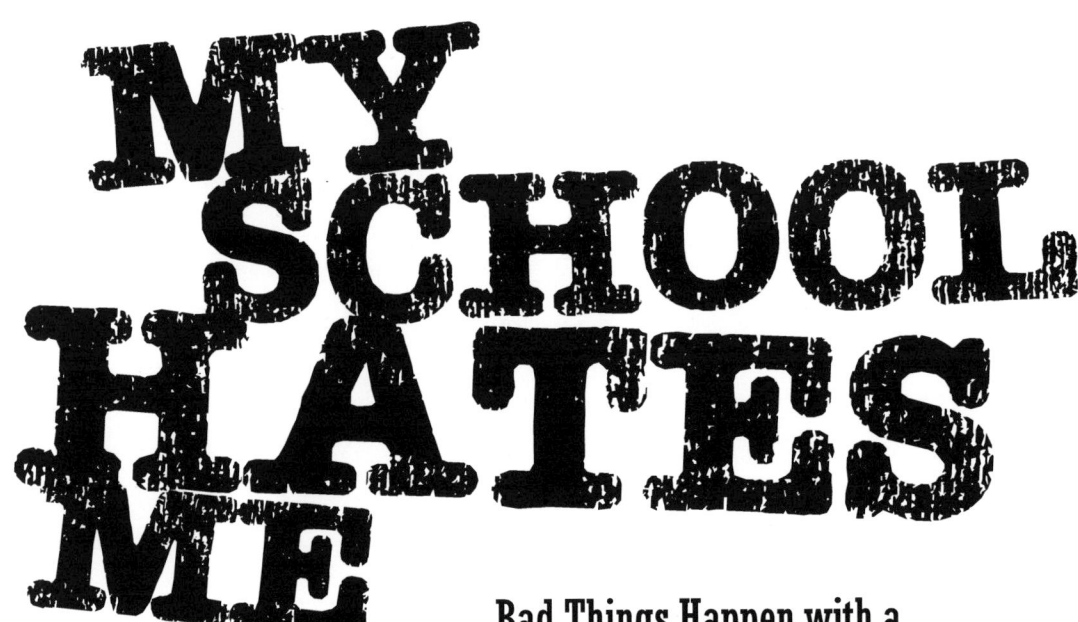

MY SCHOOL HATES ME

Bad Things Happen with a Creep in Charge

SCOUT MCCAFFREY

DEDICATION

This journal is dedicated to my 413 elementary students who deserved to be respected and fully given an opportunity to reach autonomy. I wanted to give them a voice to tell their story on how a few individuals in our school projected hatred towards them while committing the ultimate injustice of withholding education. Simultaneously, these same individuals participated in a social crushing of these very young students' self-esteem and possibly forever changed their life journey.

Hopefully, their story will help all school kids across America, and inspire educators to take action when witnessing another adult targeting a struggling student.

To my professors at Eastern Kentucky University who taught me about student advocacy and ignited my passion in the counseling field: Dr. Puglia, Dr. Stockberger, Dr. Engbretson, and Dr. Thomas.

Lastly, I am forever grateful to my own children who I love dearly and feel blessed to have in my life. The joy of being your parent is immeasurable.

Scout McCaffrey

INTRODUCTION

"Let people realize clearly that every time they threaten someone or humiliate or unnecessarily hurt or dominate or reject another human being, they become forces for the creation of psychopathology, even if these be small forces. Let them recognize that every person who is kind, helpful, decent, psychologically democratic, affectionate, and warm, is a psychotherapeutic force, even though a small one." ~ **Abraham Maslow**

Based on my personal experience, cancel culture is plainly and simply defined: There will be a winner (the perpetrator) and there will be a loser (the target). A child is never exempt and is considered equal prey from the perpetrator's perspective.

This elevated adult play is extremely diabolical in nature and has the intent to emotionally destroy a person's existence without actually physically killing them.

People who adopt this ideology are mentally compromised and have no fear of being held accountable. Their belief system is over rot with narcissism and they will use any means to win.

We have neglected addressing mental health services in our past and now the past has come to haunt us in our most sacred spaces such as a school where individuals who were once children themselves, now prey upon the same type of child who they find were as weak as they had been.

"The good life is a process, not a state of being.
It is a direction not a destination"

~ Carl Rogers

Contents

SECTION I   1

Chapter 01: Scout Mc Caffrey, Elementary School Counselor 3

Chapter 02: I Hate You Because You Exist 9

Chapter 03: The Zebra In The Room 17

Chapter 04: All Aboard 24

Chapter 05: Gap Kids 31

Chapter 06: The Predator 35

Chapter 07: The Principal Unveils His Predatory Plan 41

Chapter 08: The Predator's Protector 69

Chapter 09: Fight Back Or Surrender 73

Chapter 10: Friends Scatter 77

Chapter 11: Forming A Plan To Kill The Predator 82

Chapter 12: The Urge To Harm 88

Chapter 13: Misguided Passion 91

Chapter 14: Worldview 95

Chapter 15: Minutes Before Sandy Hook 98

SECTION II   103

Chapter 16: Resource Officers 105

Chapter 17: Gun Laws And Violence 110

Chapter 18: Neighborhood Schools 115

Chapter 19: Recess 119

Chapter 20: Medicaid 123

Chapter 21: Are We Getting Our Money's Worth? 132

Chapter 22: Vincent Van Gogh 139

Chapter 23: Counselor Role And Code Of Ethics 144

Chapter 24: Trauma Stacks Up 151

Chapter 25: How Do I Find Help? 159

Chapter 26: Please Don't Let Me Land In The Street 164

Chapter 27: Currency For The Poor.. 171

Chapter 28: Get Out And Take Another Job 177

Chapter 29: Purpose And Hope.. 184

Chapter 30: Suicide.. 187

Chapter 31: Failure 193

Chapter 32: Forgiveness... 200

Chapter 33: Scout's Blueprint For Recovery..................................... 208

SECTION I

CHAPTER 01:
SCOUT MC CAFFREY, ELEMENTARY SCHOOL COUNSELOR

"It is not difficult to deduce from an individual's position the kind of childhood he must have had. Unless something or somebody intervenes, he spends the rest of his life stabilizing his position and dealing with situations that threaten it: by avoiding them, warding off certain elements or manipulating them provocatively so that they are transformed from threats into justifications." ~ **Eric Berne**

Throughout my career, I had opportunity to counsel many students and learned how important Jean Piaget's theory of cognitive development was in describing the differences in thinking between child and adult.

If I were to truly help my students, it was important to understand how their perspective was limited by life experience along with personal interpretation of words and meaning that were potentially vastly different from their adult teachers. Piaget's theory provided a good explanation for the many classroom problems that arose out of misunderstandings between the two groups.

During student counseling sessions, I would remain open to all the hidden clues in partial statements, body language, and drawings, since each were an important part of the child's story. My adult life experiences and assumptions would be barriers if I allowed them to become part of the student's narrative.

A lot of progress was made in resolving emotional health issues when the student was given an opportunity to openly express his/her own interpretation and perception of the problem. Unfortunately, many times this did not match the teacher's impression, which would result in a conflict remaining in the classroom.

My experience allowed me to understand that children were driven naturally towards seeking equilibrium and were instinctively attuned to when balance went awry. Because elementary children are very forthcoming and want to tell their story, solution focused therapy is effective for routine problems, as the child is in search of answers and desires to make change. This theoretical orientation was introduced to me in a lecture by Dr. Gerald B. Sklare from the University of Louisville which helps children solve a problem faster by identifying realistic solutions which they can easily deploy. This method allows students to be empowered in their own therapeutic treatment by focusing on solutions instead of why the problem occurred.

The theorist Carl Rogers formed his counseling approach by offering the client "unconditional positive regard." This guideline served as the foundation for being "in the moment" with a student. Recognizing the value and courage of a child presenting themselves to a counselor during a critical moment gives unconditional respect, thus allowing them to build trust and know they are working towards a common goal of healing with a caring adult.

Carl Rogers's client-centered play therapy is the most powerful tool for utilization during a crisis. Effective work can take place with a sand tray when a child is rendered without words to express his/her concerns or is apprehensive about divulging an intimate situation.

Engaging in therapeutic play allows the child a comfortable and familiar setting to surrender in safety so they can finally express what has happened.

Unfortunately, play therapy in a school setting is highly misunderstood and interpreted as a "reward" by school staff and so its use becomes limited.

When we honor a child with respect, utilize counseling theories and practices, understand limited boundaries from life experience, and listen through a "child lens," the student is revered as worthy and enjoys membership in the school community.

This is a tall order to fill in an educational setting and can only be achieved if outlined as an important practice of school culture; otherwise, children can become easily disrespected when not offered the opportunity to truly express emotional pain in their own voice free from tainted adult misinterpretations.

School districts who prioritize strengthening the foundation of emotional health for its students create a positive school culture that is truly beneficial. This critical investment in internal nurturing during the formative years allows schools to recognize the important role it plays in building groundwork for academic and social success.

My graduate educational background consisted of learning numerous counseling theories and utilizing best evidence-based practices. I felt well-trained from my university program due to cross-referencing of different theorists in every class. We also engaged in many "live therapies" to practice what we had studied.

It was important for counselors to understand the backing of science and recognize an accepted theory; however, there was a theorist who our professors briefly discussed as an outlier because he had difficulty gathering evidence to support his hypothesis. His idea was worth noting because it was based on recognizable behavior that we have all experienced.

This psychiatrist was Eric Berne and his work involved studying human behavior and how they communicated with one another, which led to his theory of transactional analysis. His theory was controversial because it relied on subjects being honest and having the ability for introspection. Some participants studied could not recognize the impact of their own dysfunctional behavior as it created problems for others. Unfortunately, for these subjects, unhealthy childhood experiences had interfered with the appropriate development of healthy social interactions as they aged.

Berne had authored *Games People Play* in 1964, and when one reads his book, he/she can easily identify a friend, family, or acquaintance who often displays the described characteristics; however, we end up discounting their deficits as an annoyance and justify it as part of their personality that we have learned to accept or run from!

What happens when a lot of dysfunctional habits listed in his book are piled into one human being and "the game" becomes their total existence as it did when our school was invaded by a group of wayward educators?

In my desperate search for answers at the school, I noticed how this adopted play had become extremely elevated in these individuals and appeared to have developed into a personality disorder because the behaviors had now become engrained without challenge. This unfortunately created a com-monality amongst the group where they were comfortable with each other because there was no opposition to their thought. I also had noticed that a narrow lens of filtering information had emerged. These were like-minded people who thought and acted in unlikeable manners because they were unable to receive feedback from others outside their group.

As they gain experience and enjoy rewards from deception, they balance issues by replacing critical thinking with the act of dividing thoughts into two different buckets: either total acceptance with an "all in" attitude because it benefits them or "annihilation by hatred" to destroy a threat with whom they disagree.

Berne's description of internal games that people play are obvious when one tries to balance the child, adult, and parent behaviors in these individuals. Because emotional growth was seized at an early age due to some sort of trauma, they remain forever stagnant in the child part of their personality.

Since my encounter with a predatory principal and his team of followers, which I describe in this memoir, I believe these individuals fit the profile of what Berne had in mind. These are not people who engage in physical harm; they are ignited by inflicting emotional destruction on a target and enjoy with great satisfaction watching the decline of the victim's self-esteem and the eventual altering of their life.

As hard as it was for me to comprehend that a certain adult could easily target and destroy a child's chance at having success in life, it became clear when I assessed these few disrupters that they too were emotionally the same age as my students and viewed the game as restoring power and control. They were like an ordinary school bully accept they were adults with advanced diabolical skills.

I believe we have to recognize the hatred behavior of these individuals as an entity like when we inscribe on our money "In God We Trust." There may be no proof but we recognize that it may exist.

The benefits of the belief "In God We Trust" can be positively rewarding, filled with love, creativity, respect, and giving. Unfortunately, at the other end of the spectrum lies hatred where the distortive thoughts of winning are driven by annihilation and fulfilled by dominance and power.

We are surrounded by those who give and those who take but we are not prepared for those who annihilate. These are the extremes that live and work amongst us who have the outward appearance of likability, charm, and possibly good looks, but inside they are manipulators, power seekers, and fraudulent beings who make every effort to hide their real truth as they take down a target who exists in a space which they feel entitled to control.

The damaging effect of hatred inflicted on a mark is a life-altering change that has difficulty being reversed, and when predatory behavior is protected by a supervisor, it is allowed to continue unchallenged, thus leaving victims without recourse.

"Cancel culture" wasn't a mainstream term when I was a school counselor. In fact, the obscure nature and understanding of this practice is what stopped me from publishing this memoir sooner because I didn't understand what our school had gone through and it took a long time to figure out.

I was naïve to how widespread evil had penetrated our campus and exposed people who I never thought would be willing participants. The rationality for justifying the bizarre whirlwind of activity excluded common sense, ethics, and morality. There was no time for me to even catch my breath before another devious plan was enacted. There was a malignant drive for power and control that seemed to possess their being.

Imagine the destruction to one's adult life when they fall prey to being "cancelled" by a group of irrationals who are unproductive occupiers of their workplace. Now comprehend a six- or seven-year-old being delivered the same blow in their school environment. This is what happened to some of my students, and it was like witnessing a horrific accident in slow motion and I was desperately trying to save them without any skill or education in defeating this type of predatory mindset.

CHAPTER 02:
I HATE YOU BECAUSE YOU EXIST

If only I could go back in time to the exact moment of the day when I was full of life and really loved what I was doing, I would change the nanosecond of time right after that when I was in the right place but unexpectedly at the wrong time. This particular point was the exact moment someone determined my existence should be destroyed. This was the exact moment a secret plan was put in place to cancel the future of some of our students. This was the exact moment I had no idea what lay ahead when our district hired a person in charge of our school who embraces the ideology of hatred. This was the beginning where I would learn firsthand the benefits of enormous power that was achieved through "gaslighting" an entire district as a bully group of organized haters pulled off their plan undetected in our school.

When someone dislikes another, it's usually a result of an unfavorable interaction. There's possibly a stubbornness between the two along with a competitive exchange to prove one was right over the other. Having a negative historical relationship will cause these individuals to either avoid one another or hopefully have courage to listen to each other's grievance and find compromise.

On the other hand, when a person hates your existence, they don't even have to know your name or even have met you for that fact. They just perceive that you are a malignant threat and a massive obstacle in the way of their happiness. You are no different than someone driving a car in front of them on the highway. Your existence is smothering their expectations of peace and fracturing their ability to function because unbeknownst to you, you are taking away energy from their power. Your breathing carbon life serves no purpose to their superior existence nor to the fantasy world they have created for themselves, so you must be locked out of life's pleasures and rights, thus eliminating any chance you may cause them further harm.

These types of individuals can think of nothing else but vaporizing your footprint and form tunnel vision until the task is accomplished. Because they do not possess basic skills in problem-solving, they have only one tool that is finely honed to deal with your presence and that is to deploy strategies for total emotional annihilation by humiliation, ostracization, and cancellation.

This is my personal story wherein I share what I experienced and uncovered as an elementary school counselor working in a small county of Kentucky. My students needed their story told so other kids won't fall prey to academic and/or emotional targeting from toxic school staff.

Even though it has been several years since I last saw my students, they have been with me while I write our story. You see, I am an adult and could never understand how a few people were able to be so precisely destructive to another human being without conscience especially a child; therefore, how could my 413 students ever understand how their future will be affected?

Our school was a low-performing diverse institution that struggled to deliver proficient students in state assessments. We had a mid-high free and reduced rate over 70 percent, meaning almost three-fourths of our families met the federal guidelines for poverty.

Our student body included a large group of "non-performing" children (GAP students) who were receiving intervention services in reading and math for at least a year. Their family income was barely outside the federal poverty guidelines so they did not qualify for much funding. These GAP children struggled one to two years academically behind their peers, which made them targets by educators with tremendous moral deficits.

My goal with this memoir is to spread awareness regarding a hidden "behind-the-scenes" type of bullying from educators in our schools that is directed towards certain students either because of their academic failures or personality shortcomings. These few individuals that have power over whether a child receives a fair and equitable education do not care about the systemic impact their maltreatment delivers on a targeted child's school career. Furthermore, they can't even recognize the consequences of the student's eventual fallout of being rejected by their academic community at such a young age. It made me wonder if this hatred and rejection inflicted by adults could have a negative psychological effect on children that corrupts their internal dialog into thinking their school hates them.

Adult bullying directed at students by school staff is an overlooked and accepted practice academic stakeholders have failed to address and form policy or procedures to combat.

By recognizing adult bullying and the impact on the school environment, stakeholders can learn to understand how the degradation plays a role on student performance and potential disengagement from the school community. When school staff become a target as well, this creates a malignant atmosphere of paranoia in a work environment that destroys trust.

There are many children and adults who are at risk of being targeted in a low-performing school as the institution itself has already been violated by administrative neglect.

Adult bullies not only verbally assault and project their hateful behavior on a target but they can also work behind the scenes academically and emotionally targeting certain children who cause them distress.

This is a covert assault that is motivated by hate and very hard to detect because the individuals who practice this ideology work their marketing strengths in projecting likability and hide behind a façade of charm.

These individuals execute the gold standard of hatred in a school environment because they are able to weaponize their misdeeds with protection from a supervisor. Since their harm avoids leaving physical scars on a perceived target, they are able to filter hatred precisely on internal destruction of a human being without consequences.

In my opinion, this clandestine approach is a unique form of "hatred" that allowed our perpetrators to pick a specific group of "non-performing" or "misbehaved" students who were occupying a "funded" space that a more "conforming" or "better-behaved" child can utilize. These students are statistical nightmares for bully staff, and if children have protection in academic programs or behavioral plans, the bullies will seek "backdoor" ways for revenge.

These same adults who are covertly organized will target staff who appear more ethical, well-liked, or intellectually competent. They view these traits as a threat and use them as the target's weakness to be exploited in the takedown.

A school staff bully ring believes a targeted adult must be annihilated so there is no chance they can expose the incompetency of the players in the ring. They also believe targeted children do not deserve the right to be educated if they continuously fail to show progress or disrupt the classroom.

These individuals operate on intently exhibiting bias-motivated hatred in their quest for power and control of individuals they deem a threat because it is natural to them. They will never be accountable for their stake in decimating a target nor can they comprehend the impact of their actions on the academic and emotional health of a child because they lack the ability to even care about "cause and effect." The narrow filter of hate gives these unhinged individuals "deserving pleasure" when performing unethical misdeeds, so they see no wrong in their action even if multiple sources confront them to state they are being unjust.

A "hostile school culture" can create a broken emotional foundation in a child, resulting in loss of "hope and purpose" especially where they fit in their school community. As I watched the deterioration of order in our elementary school that final year, I wondered if "hatred" introduced by adult bullying could be instrumental in setting the seeds of "hatred" in children when they lose trust and no longer feel accepted or safe in the school setting. Does a broken school culture translate to the potential of targeted children becoming violent down the road? If so, how can we encourage educational environments to look inward and reflect on the health of their culture and its effect on the very persons who are a part of their school?

A toxic teacher can effectively increase the odds a child will not thrive while in their classroom. This negative school experience can render the student in a downward unrecoverable spiral simply because learning had been halted and their self-esteem fractured with continued negative reinforcement.

A toxic non-learning environment can deliver a negative paradigm shift in a child that can become life-changing and detrimental to their well-being. I believe this extreme shift can create a dramatic change in their worldview as the relentless negative school experience shapes them to accept low self-worth and feelings of rejection. I feel they become at risk from their emotional trauma, so could easily justify violence or personal destruction because they were forced to accept a life of unworthiness from an environment which they should have been able to trust.

A school can and should be part of a student's resiliency package, which includes learning protective factors such as an empathetic response, problem-solving abilities, decision-making skills, regulating impulse control, planning and organizational skills. Learning to work as a team and develop conflict resolution skills are all protective factors that can have a profound impact on keeping a child upright and stable as they journey throughout life. These developmental tasks are best accomplished through partnership with the parent and a positive educational environment that exhibits a healthy school culture. When these conditions are not met, trust, safety, and a sense of belonging can diminish.

A school is a sacred space, and adults or other deviant people who violate the sanctity of such a protected environment need to be stopped, removed, and prosecuted from ever being near children.

I believe every school district in our nation has ignored or accepted incidents of adult bullying from certain staff on their students and/or employees. My story not only involves students who were targeted but myself as well for trying to protect them.

There is no inoculation against controlling the impulsive, or planned, act of someone who wants to commit hateful acts, but there are some areas that may help in the prevention of this type of personal assault if we could understand the environment in which this is allowed to happen.

By discovering the toxicity and incompetency's that have penetrated the school culture, we can then formulate policies and standards to protect our students and staff from a disastrous outcome.

If we understand pathology plays a role in hateful behavior, then we know there must be urgency in taking necessary action to countereffect the damage.

Progress begins with acknowledging and educating top leadership including the human resources department on the serious mental health harm that can come to a school and its occupants especially when the perpetrator is given a leadership role over children or staff.

When we develop protective rights for targets, we are offering them protection from victimization. When we allow witnesses to freely come forward without retaliation, we are allowing them to expose pathology. When we hold leadership accountable, we are ensured of a healthy school or workplace environment. All are necessary safety measures for protecting targeted children and adults who have been victimized by this type of attack.

With proper attention to policies, rights, and oversight we can expect to see a reduction in targeted persons when covert predatory behavior will become more difficult to achieve. This is how we give targets a voice and this is how we keep our environments safer.

Witnesses of adult bullying directed towards students or other staff must have the courage to step forward and act when human rights are violated without regard for their own career or self, so effective change can take place. This bold ability to be called to action when it is ethically and morally right could truly have a significant impact on a child's future and help retain talented staff.

It is also important that laws to protect children from harm in a school setting allow prosecution of those in power who choose to protect known predatory behavior when it is brought to their attention. Supervisors must be required to report to authorities so an appropriate independent investigation can be accomplished by trained professionals who can identify the behavior and its impact on the student and/or employee. A supervisor who is an active participant of the alleged crime cannot be part of the investigation.

As those with dysfunctional teaching goals gain more access to power from a toxic culture, our talented staff who have transferred to better school environments unfortunately create a vacuum of students with high academic and emotional needs ultimately footing the bill. The chances of a student being placed in a nurturing positive classroom diminishes with the rising turnover rate of these most talented teachers.

An organized hate group in a school setting can involve many actors. It only requires one leader and the crucial protection from someone in power, such as a superintendent, in order to thrive.

"I hate you because you exist" is internal dialog that a hater forms to justify their attack. Hate doesn't require a logical reason and is always clear in who is intended as target. They have nothing but disdain for the intended victim simply because they exist in a space they want to control, and that is all the motive they need.

CHAPTER 03:
THE ZEBRA IN THE ROOM

This chapter is for those who have never been a target of extreme hatred. I offer my direct personal experience to hopefully help one understand the mindset of an irregular individual and how they can easily function in the school.

In order to totally grasp the internal dialog of this hater, I had to quash my own abilities like common sense, ethics, and accountability. It was not easy, as these skills were innate and served me well up until I crossed paths with my new principal. There is no room in the hater's business model or game plan that involves any other higher-order skills such as critical thinking, perspective taking, and self-awareness. It was imperative to understand all of these skills were absent in this hater's repertoire.

Prior to the encounter, I had limited experience with the framework of this extreme mindset in a work setting nor did I completely understand the depth of their workings. Had I been lucky during my past employment to avoid such a personally destructive encounter, or did my naivety finally deserve a wake-up call that almost every successful hardworking individual will eventually fall prey to this unregulated extreme behavior?

Unfortunately, in the beginning I thought it was me personally that was under attack even though I had never met the man before. Since I had no history with him, maybe he heard complaints from someone else so I needed to prove that my skills were beyond his expectations and that I just had to work harder. This was a mistake on my part as I wasted a lot of time trying to prove my work was valuable instead of focusing on the fact that I was actually chosen as the target of a private ambush.

In the summer prior to the new academic year starting, I had received a clear message from my new principal that he was intentionally avoiding me. The unsettledness and massive disruption to my role as school counselor gave urgency to gain more insight into what his goals were with our students and myself. His contradictory management style was a key indicator that my employment was drastically going to change. "Why is this happening?"

It had become clear that if our paths might accidently cross, he would take great pains to avoid an encounter. He was an enigma, and I was a deplorable person that appeared to him as some type of contaminate. He mostly kept a distance from me as he blew about the school never lighting anywhere long enough where I could attempt a conversation.

He did not fit the impression of an adult-in-charge because he lacked leadership engagement. I wasn't seeing any contributions during staff meetings like other principals. He would be seated like a distant bystander, disengaged with his head continuously facing down, scribbling in a notepad.

The first thing that came to my mind was this guy was definitely an "elephant in the room," as I felt seasoned staff were probably thinking the same when they often looked in his direction expecting some type of interaction.

We have all heard of the saying "the elephant in the room," and sometime during our life, we have to face a big problem that no one wants to confront. It definitely makes most people uncomfortable and puts us in a situation we rather avoid but can't because it affects one's life.

I felt very uncomfortable in his presence because of the unknown and wanted to uncover the barrier that divided us. I figured knowing the "reasons" would be a good starting point to repairing the relationship because I had no idea on how it was broken in the first place.

Thinking of the "elephant in the room" situation, and although its meaning matched the circumstances, it didn't exactly provide me answers on how to deal with my concern because this animal was at the head of the adult table with enormous power, yet there he sat quietly disengaged acting as if he were at the kiddie table. I was stymied at the "never before seen" obstacle before me and perplexed at how to make a connection under such odd conditions that seemed to be his normal.

The color gray an elephant represents symbolically stuck out to me as a neutral standpoint between black and white. Being unbiased would allow unfettered ideas to flow for the best plan of action in dealing with the problem at hand. Curbing any unfair judgment formed of him, I had to figure out how to understand the "foreign language" his body was using for communication instead of active mature engagement.

Stepping back, I wanted to observe how effective other staff were in their ability to receive a response from him. It was hard to find examples because he was standoffish with most except for a few in his tight circle who would inappropriately giggle and whisper during their conversations. The immature group reminded me of our students when they wanted to share a secret and would shush each other when a "non-member" approached.

Because we worked in the office together, I tried different options to engage him in conversation but it had an opposite effect that made him distance himself further. I became an invisible bystander just observing his interactions with others and noticed the words he delivered were convincing and showed such care. If I had been directly in the conversation, I would have believed what he was saying but because I was at a watchful distance,

I could easily see the repetition of words used with each encounter. He had developed a vocabulary of comforting language that others would enjoy hearing and because of that they could easily form an opinion that he really cared.

The beautiful words he spoke were all lies and his behaviors became his truths, but most people who encountered him lost sight of the whole picture after the words were delivered. This is what honest people do when they still have trust for their fellow man.

He was an arrogant machine spewing "word vomit" to others with no intent to actually follow through. As he told them how much their needs were going to be met out of one corner of his mouth, he was further from the truth on the opposite side.

Convincing "easy marks" he was genuine was part of the game when in actuality he had no ambition to ever help another human being unless it served his purpose.

When listeners felt goose bumps from his beautiful words, it made it easy to hide the warning of hair that was probably standing up on the back of their necks.

His faulty thinking was a well-thought-out plan designed to depict him as a hero. He was going to save others from these horrible problems in our school that he and only he is brave enough to face. What they didn't know was he was the one who created the problems. There was no questioning of him on intent, and challenges were met with abrupt temper tantrums that became twisted and projected on a target. He would propagandize to witnesses how the target was to blame for igniting his passion to "rescue children," and so the word vomit continued. What a magician he is showing to be that distracts with one hand while tricking with the other.

Everyone was a pawn that played a role in his elevated game that was so complex and intertwined that it was impossible to follow one distraction because he had created another diversion on top of it that was just as complicated. These were nothing but mousetraps designed to divert from what he was trying to hide, and the simplistic way in which he categorized people helped me realize that he was not an "elephant in the room" but a "zebra in the room!"

I had it wrong and had wasted my time trying to find a narrative of "normal common behaviors" fit an abnormal person who brilliantly delivered a one-way communication that fed his ability to effectively con others.

He was simple in his thinking and categorized everything into "black or white," "good or bad." Every behavior projected from him was approached from a "reward or punishment" perspective towards a person. It was "all or nothing," so anything in between wasn't an option. There was no listening to others, no compromise, no perspective taking, he was the only one allowed to speak, and it was backed up by his authority of being a principal. He effectively "locked out" giving rights to anyone who wasn't him, and those who became his followers for the time being were handsomely rewarded by having their incompetency protected. This methodical way of dividing staff allowed those who lacked critical thinking and autonomy to be rewarded as "useful servants" and those with skills and talent to be punished through intense harassment and character assassination.

This extreme way of thinking is what I now believe groomed his narrow filter that easily allowed "hatred" of those to be placed in his "bad bucket" and become targets.

It finally made sense that my confused impression of him was in expecting higher-order thinking which I now know he was completely incapable of even possessing because of his social deficits. He had pruned effective communication skills and empathy for others from his mind at an earlier age.

21

I was dealing with narcissistic young childlike thinking, and it answered why he was rigid and unapproachable. The life he saw for others was based on his perception of what they deserved.

This "zebra man-child" was a total black-and-white animal with defined lines that had no gray. I would come to learn his world and understand why he thought some students had no "right to be educated" and why I had no "right to earn a living" or experience "free will." He was in charge of oppressing our unworthy lives and we belonged in his "bad bucket" to be destroyed.

Because most haters identify themselves as a victim through some sort of trauma that was inflicted during their earlier life span, they believe they are owed restitution by seeking revenge on another to restore power lost. In other words, their victimhood was payment for not being accountable for their hateful behavior. They survive by lying, deceitfulness, and bullying in order to hide the broken person they really are inside.

The communication relationship between a target and a narcissist are two parallel lines that will never intersect because the target's worldview includes empathy and the narcissist's worldview only includes himself.

Unfortunately, some of us were now in the hands of a person who had direct intent to pursue his own ideological agenda and destroy anyone who dared to stop him. He had pathological traits and he had power.

I had been thrown into a yearlong "zebra microcosm" of feeling and seeing the effects of his predatory behavior. I had never opened this part of my thinking before, and now after witnessing all his capricious acts, it was all over my head and it was evil.

Only a person who has been a direct target of hatred understands and recognizes the profound effect the experience can have on changing the trajectory of one's life.

The predator's faulty thinking had been groomed in early childhood and his skill set to defend its problem created for others was well elevated and polished by the time he became an adult. Because hatred had been so pervasive in his thoughts, it was confused as a higher order skill when in actuality it was a maladaptive coping mechanism for untreated personality deficits.

I often wondered what the outcome would have been had this principal been identified early in life and received counseling intervention. Would so many children and adults have been negatively affected by his childhood issues if it wasn't ignored and allowed to grow to a full-blown personality disorder in adulthood?

As a child, he learned to simplify life stressors in black-and-white terms. It made it easier for him to be a "zebra thinker" when he became an adult because higher-order skills unfortunately failed to arrive. By then, anyone who didn't think like him lived in a "foreign world" that only "deplorable humans" navigate, and he believes they must be destroyed when they become a threat.

CHAPTER 04:
ALL ABOARD

My best description of how our toxic school culture worked in targeting students is outlined in the following allegory:

It was like riding a train. Here we go down the tracks at X miles per hour. The school principal is the conductor. He regulates the speed, fuel, stops, and appearance of the train. The conductor has complete power and organizes which students are assigned to certain cars based on statistical information.

Up front in the first car are the gifted and talented students. They enjoy lots of first-class amenities such as individual cubicles, enrichment activities, and the best technology. The car is beautifully tailored to their academic growth.

You probably won't see our "gifted" actively engaged with one another because that is too much competition and could threaten their gifted status if one outdid the other. We also have to ignore social issues with "non-gifted" peers because their parents have told us they just have difficulty communicating with kids their own age and prefer to be around adults.

These highly talented students bring us honor and school recognition for their high academic achievements and that we can measure. It allows us to take credit and easily ignore their need for social improvement because that we do not measure. Unfortunately, we do notice they have increased anxiety, but doesn't everybody?

In the next car are proficient performers. They are spot on for grade level and on track for academic growth. They make us proud too, and each year we honor our "proficient" along with the "gifted and talented" in a formal schoolwide ceremony with medals to recognize their achievement in making our school district proud. The proficient students are mostly well balanced academically and socially with their peers.

In the third car are GAP students. They can't fit in the same car as their proficient peers because they are behind academically for their grade level. Some may receive intervention services in reading and math after a lengthy documentation period, but it also depends on teacher support in pushing the idea through. There will be lots of meetings on these kids that involve a team of staff to determine their academic needs and complete the documentation process.

GAP kids will require the teacher to present a differentiated lesson plan more tailored to their level from other students in the class. This is a time-consuming process for a teacher alone to be responsible, as they have to direct more one-on-one attention to this student as they balance the regular lessons with the rest of the class.

This distribution of time is like asking a teacher to put both feet on opposite ends of a teeter-totter and keep their entire class upright for the day without dipping one way or the other. Sometimes they fall off altogether because they are presented with an ethical dilemma of either helping the student who has the most needs or continue working with their classmates, who, as a group, offer more children who can be serviced by their teaching and produce a more favorable statistical outcome.

These GAP kids won't fit in the next car either because they don't qualify for special education services. They may not have a recognized diagnosis of a disability or the point difference between their IQ and academic output is not large enough. They also may not have behavioral deficits. If you looked from outside the train car, they appear well behaved, but if you were inside the car, you might think they were "daydreaming" and wishing they were somewhere else.

These children are an anomaly and remain a mystery to every school in America. I believe these students have high emotional needs that have never been addressed because their ability to just get by is usually not accompanied by bad behavior. They often are labeled as "not motivated" or possibly "learned helplessness," and we don't have any academics programs that fit those needs; therefore, we have to find ways to shuffle them around without anyone noticing. The last car on the train would be good for them as this is where we put the "I don't know what program this kid belongs to and it will only be temporary!"

GAP students are the most vulnerable for toxic school cultures to fudge their growth because there are so many of them and few "funded" spots available. If the school can show they are making progress, they can pop them up to the car with the "proficient" students and they can physically blend in with their peers.

The data will have to be falsified to bump them up to their peer proficient car, which is not a problem when you have a conductor of the train that is out for his own notoriety. Why he has a whole team of test takers; unfortunately, they happen to be teachers who would love to get rid of the "little non-performer" that just can't appreciate their "perfect teaching methods."

In the fourth car are special education students that may have academic or behavioral deficits. Their train ride provides space with less students, as well as extra support staff and guidelines for federal and state protection.

The school receives extra funding to offset the costs, which allow the students to have their needs met most appropriately because they have legal oversight from the government.

Lastly is the caboose where the school counselor is stationed to keep an eye on every passenger car and especially wants to make sure all children are afforded the opportunity to be successful academically and emotionally. It is most important every kid knows they are a valuable part of the school community.

The last car will start to fill up midyear as students are re-evaluated and their performance is not up to par. Some of them have "lost qualifications" from programs they were initially assigned. They will be flagged, evaluated, studied, and eventually sent to the back of the train as an outlier until the school can figure out where to place them.

A scrambling effect will take place on pushing the parent to do something with their non-performer as well. We might encourage a medical evaluation to see if something like that may be interfering or maybe inquire if they have a medication issue that might be the answer. Maybe something different has happened at home. The school comforts the parent by expressing they have tried everything for their child to learn, and so they will present evidence showing their child's lack of progress. The parent interprets that differently, such as the teacher isn't interested in meeting their child's needs or the teacher is always hostile towards their child because every day after school the kid comes home complaining about how their teacher hates them.

The situation has now become a "lit fuse" between the parent and school on who is accountable. If the parent is disengaged altogether, then the child can easily stay in the back car until other students are addressed first.

The longer the student remains in the back car, the chances of them moving up to the car with their peers is more unlikely. Eventually, the last car will fill up fast and start to wobble on the journey down the track. The wheels begin to wear down and grind from the weight of so many students who are secretly packed into the small space.

As the train makes its way through the community with its brightly colored cars, it becomes noticeable the last car is not looking too good. Not only are the wheels wobbly and searching the rails but the paint is peeling and showing wear because the school didn't invest in high grade paint for that car like they did for the others.

You can see children's little fingers poking through the knotholes of the car as they try to claim air from so many kids packed in together. They are sort of smiling with many faces squished against the glass as puffs of breath expand and contract on the window. These students are somewhat curious on where they are going.

Unfortunately, as the train is meandering through town, the conductor receives a complaint from the school board, "You must do something with that last car, it's embarrassing." At first the conductor decides to board up the windows and patch the knotholes so no one sees what is happening inside, but the car still looks bad.

He then decides to paint the boards and knothole imperfections a wonderful color like the rest of the train. As the train makes its way back around to the school board for another showing, there are no more complaints. In fact, the school board even compliments the conductor on his work and how much they love the beautiful paint. It truly shows he is working on the problem and cares about his students.

Unfortunately, after passing the school board and receiving lots of praise, the last car continues to fill up as the train makes its way around the outskirts of town. The wheels continue to wobble and screeching noises are once again heard. The car is grossly overloaded and dragging the train down. The conductor feels he must get rid of some of the weight it's distracting from the front cars that look so glorious.

The kids in the back car have no oversight, so he concocts a great idea. "Let's throw out their books, pencils, desks, and any school items that would help them learn because they are not learning anyway!"

As the train continues down the track, the rails are littered with educational debris but no one notices because like a kid who doesn't want to eat his peas, he spreads the trash out. The wheels are not screeching anymore but they are still wobbly; he must do something drastic before they loop back towards the school board again. He wants more praise!

Since he was already two steps ahead in his plan to deceive that stupid school board, the conductor decides to stop the train in the middle of nowhere so no one can see what he was about to do.

He makes his way to the last car, and with a warm smile, politely orders the non-performers to disembark. He reassures the kids by announcing, "No worries, someone will pick you up later."

The students sensing something wasn't right look to the school counselor who pleads, "Don't do it … it's a trap! Interlock your arms and make a human chain!" The students scramble and lock their arms together as they refuse to leave the car.

The conductor is not even bothered by their reaction, and he actually chuckled at how stupid the kids are acting, so his smirky eyes connect with the counselor as she is viewed just the same. He had already preplanned this desolate stop with a way to lure the children to their final destination, so he points out a beautiful playground they could see off in the distance.

He mentions the toys, bicycles, and footballs that everyone can enjoy. The students stare for a moment at all the goodies the conductor had left for them but still have a slight sense something is wrong, so refuse to leave the car.

The school counselor frantically begs them to stay put but the conductor has one last ace in the hole. You see he had a big, huge bag of candy, lots of candy. This was his trademark; he always had a stash of candy and had been grooming the kids with these treats since he started at the school. Kids love candy, and they love him because he unconditionally supplied it freely throughout the school day all year long.

The conductor had earned their trust from this one simple act of "kindness" and eventually lured the students out of the car one by one as they unlocked arms and filled their hands with treats. They were happy for the moment as they skipped to the beautiful playground and tried out all the toys.

After the last child steps off, the conductor then orders the train to quickly press forward as he waves good-bye to the students and shouts with a warm charming face, "The middle school train will be here to pick you up soon!"

The school counselor weeps in her car alone, afraid what the future would now hold for her students. They had become the next class of throwaways who had been rejected by their school community because no one could figure out how to help them.

This, unfortunately, is the end of the story for some children on their educational journey.

CHAPTER 05:
GAP KIDS

What are GAP kids? It depends on which educator you ask and their interpretation. Like so many "categorizations of children" in the education field, giving clear definitions and guiding principles that are universal in nature don't exist.

By the time you interpret federal law down to state law, down to county law, down to district policies, a lot of gibber-gabber innuendos and "don't you know what that means" come flying out to see who understands or doesn't comprehend what determines a GAP designated child and who is responsible for them.

The education system has cornered the market on acronyms, and most educators could not even tell you what the actual initials mean. The good news is there are pages and pages of interpretations, ideas, and cures in every district that make someone in the educational field very happy they could help.

My understanding after asking several administrators, was that GAP kids are those students whose families do not meet the federal guidelines for free and reduced and are not performing to the standards of the proficient students in their peer group. They do not have a qualifying medical disability, and the GAP between their IQ and reading or math competency is not enough to qualify for special education services. They have won the lottery on not fitting into any protected education program.

Their minimal growth on assessments places them in an educational abyss with educators continually scrambling to figure out a solution to help these students because, ultimately, they are responsible for them on testing outcomes.

This type of child can easily become a soft target for predatory school staff when district accountability is measured by student performance, and they continually lag in growth.

These children fed the appetite of hatred with our new principal. He viewed GAP students as "Garbage and Pasture!" These students needed to be disposed of and put into an academic area where statistically they cannot harm his reputation.

Unfortunately, there is not much opportunity for schools to receive funding for these children; therefore, they can easily become a "Rubik's Cube" of experimentation, disorganized ideas, and dead-end programs as educators try to make a connection that is viable.

The lack of growth and frustration amongst school personnel can contribute to teacher disengagement with these complicated low-performing students.

Educators have described and divided these kids by socioeconomic status, race, and test scores in order to fix the problem, but the commonality they all share is lacking the same opportunities as their proficient peers and/or may have untreated emotional health issues. Because they are likeable children and do not display any outward behavioral problems, we can't recognize or pinpoint the issue on why they can't perform.

Educators become exhausted as they cycle through various attempts to promote learning and still no growth. They can easily surmise it appears these children are simply incapable of making progress. In other words, information goes in one ear and out the other!

Most of these students come from the working poor, single family, or displaced households that are good people trying to earn a living to keep their family afloat. A GAP student's life experience and availability of enriched activities are limited by their family resources. They live at the cusp of having their basic human needs met and poverty.

These are my kids who have an easier time accepting their school situation, as they have a clear understanding of how far behind they are in the classroom. It's like they're running a race each day starting further and further from the start line as their peers build a lead that can't be caught. These kids know they will have extreme difficulty catching up with their classmates and more than likely feel there is no chance of ever winning. Eventually, the drive they once had diminishes and a negative cycle of "why bother" takes over motivation.

The critical opportunity for effective intervention was needed way prior to the failure in academics, but no one in the school was able to pick up the critical signs of distress beyond failing test scores. Because of the delay in receiving appropriate counseling, the problem has now progressed into a learning issue. Unfortunately, with some students, another school year becomes repetitively unproductive. When you add the final rejection of educators who target them as "throwaways" at such a tender age, it's a devastating future for any child to ever overcome.

We are dealing with a "whole child;" therefore, it would benefit the school community to start recognizing what they can't easily see and explore the concept of *Self Determination Theory* as a best evidenced-based approach if we truly want to help these children unlock barriers to learning. These kids bring enriched value to the school community and are well worth investment. We simply need higher-order educators who can nurture their unique situation that is beyond applying academic methods for helping. It is imperative to rescue all our young citizens and especially hold those accountable who wish to toss them aside.

CHAPTER 06:
THE PREDATOR

During my work as a school counselor, I was finishing up a second master's degree to become a licensed mental health counselor. There was a need to provide clinical services to our students, as referring to outside agencies was becoming increasingly difficult due to the lack of available Medicaid providers. Children live in the "here and now"; therefore, counseling in the school environment would benefit them immensely.

One night while I was attending class, I had a chance to speak with my professor during the break about concerns with the new principal. I truly did appreciate and needed her mentorship for my perplexing situation, as it felt there was no time to waste.

After giving a brief background with example behaviors the principal utilized to avoid me, I expressed how we had gone most of the summer never meeting. In fact, I had no idea what he even looked like. I had sent emails, left messages, and wanted to introduce myself and especially welcome him to our school.

His avoidance was very concerning as the summer was time to develop programs and define the principal/counselor team. None of that happened and the school break was fading fast. It felt as if a principal had never arrived. He seemed to be a ghost with possible sightings but no physical connection to the administrative function or desire to plan the school year for our students.

I further exclaimed to my professor that we finally did meet late summer because I had a lucky break in tracking him down. The encounter was not what I expected. It was obvious I had caught him off guard, and he was even hesitant to shake my hand after introducing myself.

He acknowledged that he had received my emails and responded with, "One day we will have a meeting to discuss plans for the school year," and I told him how I looked forward to it. I did have a pressing question that needed to be addressed, as the situation timeline was coming up. I quickly asked my question, and he responded by stating that I no longer needed to worry about that task as he reassigned it to a teacher. I thought that was odd but it was a minor duty, so I accepted the change. I had no idea that there were going to be even more drastic changes as the days progressed. Next, he separated me from my students, then the parents. "What is going on?" I thought. This decision was very serious. I have to work with my students and their parents, that is why my position exists and is exactly why I chose the profession. I was extremely distraught by this incomprehensible change and didn't understand what drove him to take such a radical move.

The school secretary was a friend of the principal that he brought with him, so she gladly complied with his directive to send any counseling kid's or parent's inquiries to him for handling.

The hostile atmosphere he created also made me feel like I was being stalked at the school because anytime I left my office, he would appear within moments and interrupt my conversations. He was completely in control of my whereabouts at all times. My total existence was systematically being extinguished by my new boss.

I further noted to my professor I had concern as well about the bags of candy he kept in his office. He used it as a treat for students who were in trouble and had been removed from the classroom. He also gave these same students hand held electronic devices to play video games throughout their stay in the office. Bribery was an effective tool for him to use to keep kids quiet.

After the professor carefully listened to more incidents I recalled with students, she quietly spoke and stated, "Predator." I was taken aback and asked her to repeat what she said, and of course, I did hear it right. She had referred to my new principal as a "predator." I thought she was too harsh. I figured she didn't understand what I was saying about him, and maybe I had been too dramatic in my description.

After class, another classmate and I discussed what she said, and we both agreed that neither one of us may have enough professional counseling experience to understand the dynamics of a true predator.

Although, I didn't recognize at the time when I sought my professor's advice, that because she had accumulated valuable life experience compiled with her upper education and counseling experience, it allowed her to iden- tify the behaviors appropriately and in a precise manner. I also remember her saying to me with the most concerned look, "He has to be stopped … this man should not be in a school setting, especially around children." I thought to myself, there is nothing I can do because he is my boss, so I felt I was still at square one with my situation. After all, I was seeking advice on what I could do better in connecting with him in hopes of repairing our broken relationship where I had felt somehow accountable.

The other student in class that night who had joined our conversation was a school psychologist. Unknown to me, she actually had direct experience with the "predator" from his prior school, and when I had described what I was experiencing, she said his name and asked if he was the individual I was referring too. I was shocked that just by describing someone and also the fact that we were nearly hundred miles away from where he worked, she knew his name.

What were the odds that this "predator" had made his way to cross both our paths and allowed us to form an independent opinion he was extremely off? Could both of us be wrong and could my professor be wrong?

The school psychologist also directly told me I was going to be fired. She stated he would be terminating me because he has a "friend" he wants for his counselor, and their school had refused to hire her. She further elaborated, "He ran our former counselor off because he claimed she didn't do any work." She continued on, "Our school was in turmoil a whole year with him, and we were confused but glad when he abruptly left."

This statement of course devastated me, as I did not want to be fired; furthermore, I was concerned with why the counselor didn't do any work. I thought that was very odd because of how busy I normally was with the same job.

This new principal wasn't demonic looking nor did I think of him as a killer, which is the most extreme predator that I could think of when I heard that title. I didn't even think he was anywhere near the description of what I thought was a predator.

My "predator" knowledge was deeply incomplete and tainted by media influence. There didn't appear to be a physical attack; it was just unethical. I felt the need to control my own moral values so as to not allow unreasonable judgment towards the situation.

Work environments throughout my career were pretty much the same when it came to drama in the workforce. There is always someone who gossips, someone who is lazy, someone who is angry, someone who has their job because of connections, and someone who is not qualified.

Like my coworkers, we would sometimes complain amongst ourselves but for the most part ignore and put an arm's length distance from the dysfunction. I realize now that even though these individuals were a pain in the butt, they were a "luxury" to work with in comparison to the "predator."

He did not look like the worst of worst. He was rather ordinary looking and some could say he was handsome, and his personality exuberated "charm" allowing individuals to form an opinion he was likeable.

After my conversation with the professor, I went home and started reviewing the Diagnostic Statistical Manual (DSM). It would take weeks of observing him and lots of researching articles for me to accept the fact that when I noticed his behavior and compared his words and actions, he displayed a lot of traits that matched antisocial personality disorder or narcissistic personality disorder. I did not have the qualifications to diagnose him, but clearly being aware of a potential condition should help me survive working with him so I thought. He was a toxic person in my work environment who intentionally wanted to cause harm, and I needed a defense.

Unfortunately, I was left to fend for myself in trying to unthread the nonsense but found it quite difficult because the deeper I dove into trying to make sense of his irrational beliefs, the more it required distance from my own belief system. I would have to be cautious not to become him if I wanted to understand his evil world. To keep myself upright, I didn't have to accept his faulty thinking as right; I only had to accept that I was alone in my thoughts that it was wrong.

All the madness of his acts served as a diversion to pull me into different rabbit holes that had no escape. He wanted to keep me mindlessly busy defending myself to distract from noticing the children he was moving around in his shell game. I had to protect my 413 students from this man but had no plan on how to achieve such a feat when the odds were so very much against all of us.

Every day, I showed up at the school and became more emotionally wounded like a battered woman who stays in a bad marriage for the kids. I couldn't envision the future and how my decision to stay until the end of my contract was going to be so detrimental to my own emotional well-being.

The painful reality was I couldn't differentiate what was the lesser of two evils: walking out and abandoning my students or leaving them with a person I thought was destroying their future.

The end game was we were all going to lose except the predator. He was guaranteed to win.

CHAPTER 07:
THE PRINCIPAL UNVEILS
HIS PREDATORY PLAN

In the beginning, I had heard good things about the person who was going to be our new principal. Before he arrived, there was a repetitive buzz in the air from a few supporters exclaiming admiration for his leadership, but I also heard "clouded" opinions from other staff. In anticipation of his arrival, rumors had spread through the academia grapevine that experienced teachers at our school were hurriedly making plans for transfer to other schools in our district, as they refused to work under his administration.

When inquiring with those who seemed to be his advocate, I asked what they liked most about this new administrator, and each person regurgitated the exact same response. "He's a good principal because he knows every student's name" (as if that was something unique). Anyone who works in the office of a school knows each and every student, their siblings, and their parents. I thought it odd that these few individuals offered such a trivial standard for leadership. Wasn't anyone curious like I was about new programs or ideas he would bring to our school that will help our students succeed?

This new principal had been in our district before as a vice-principal at the nearby feeder preschool. A triggering event occurred during his employ, as the principal over him sought retirement midyear. He viewed the resignation as a perfect opportunity to move into a much sought-after position of leading a school; however, the superintendent did not feel he was the right candidate due to his lack of experience, so she recommended the position be filled with an outside candidate.

Being passed over for a promotion definitely had an impact on his career as well as sparking whispers throughout the district about his social awkwardness. The rejection was viewed by him as a humiliating lack of respect and ignited an impulsive response to leave the preschool midyear as well. He was able to obtain a position as a principal in a distant county far enough away from our district that would give him the experience needed.

When he arrived at his new school, he was able to feel the security of power through leadership as a principal for the very first time. This exuberance was crippled somewhat as he was now in uncharted territory with no familiar people in the school to serve as a layer of protection. He had learned all that he wanted to know in life, so receiving or developing new skills were not considered as they weren't necessary. Because of these deficits, his plan was to ride out in a powerful position with minimum oversight and have the right staff in place that could easily be manipulated into following his lead no matter where he took them.

The first order of business and the only important task starting at his new school was to immediately take haste in attacking the school counselor's position because they would be the one who worked side by side with him and would know his policies and work ethics. The chain of events he put in place for this attack was a precursor for what he would later inflict on me. He would begin his fight to win a position for a "friend" who needed a counseling position and fit the bill of being very loyal to him.

At the start of the school year, he swiftly launched a negative attack of the sitting counselor by taking away most of her job duties without informing staff, parents, or other stakeholders. This gave the perception that she was lazy and not doing her job, when in actuality she was probably distraught and trying to figure out why a principal would abruptly wipe out counseling services for children. What was his purpose of "window dressing" by having a counselor yet not allowing them to be an important service for the school?

The counselor had no idea what "predatory behavior" he was going to unleash on her throughout the school year nor did she even consider the fact that her career would soon be over after his intentional dismantling of her job duties and diligent campaign against her reputation.

Even the school secretary was integral to his plan. She was ordered to transfer calls or inquiries regarding the counselor to him for handling. By him effectively withholding information from the counselor, it allowed others to believe she was inattentive to the students, teachers, and parent needs, thus smearing her reputation further.

His manipulative skills allowed him to diabolically reframe the perception to stakeholders that the counselor was "incompetent and lazy." His charm and young good looks also worked to his advantage, as it dissolved any judgment from those who might for a moment question the new viewpoint.

His strategic tactics dovetailed smoothly, as the "new packaging" allowed others to forget all the "good works" done previously by the counselor. They easily adopted his perception since they were actually witnessing her "lack of engagement" towards duties. Her behavior validated what he had put in motion. No person in a school setting would have ever expected a principal to take away all duties from the school counselor, so his plan was genius.

After a long-drawn-out school year, he was successful in terminating the standing counselor but, unfortunately, had not achieved hiring his "friend" because of a critical mistake in forgetting to manipulate the Site-Based Decision-Making Council. They had turned down his pick by deciding to hire a different counselor who offered more experience.

For a second time, he became rejected. There was no way he could bluff his way through another school year since he had not introduced any new policies or plans and he certainly didn't have any idea what new programs to bring. He had spent his first year completely focused on removing a threat, and his effort only yielded half his plan. Without having a key person to serve as a "protector," his career could not move forward because the risk of being exposed as incompetent was too high; therefore, he would have to move on to another school.

Now for a second time, he was forced to abruptly leave his position, so he scurried back to our county where he had originally started his career. His resume could offer more "alleged experience" now that he had a "principal" title to prove he had acquired status to that level.

Unfortunately, our school was the only one in the district with an open position that would exactly meet his requirements. Sadly, this is when our paths crossed and I too had no idea what lay ahead.

He came to my school defeated from making critical mistakes. Instead of recognizing that his destructive actions were morally wrong, he interpreted the failure as a lack of attention to be more forceful with the council. The intense isolation felt at that school also made him acutely aware that he required comfort from other like-minded individuals who were devout followers. Having a team would provide ego nurturing as well as unconditional positive reinforcement of his toxic ideas.

His new plan had to be more detailed and conscious of identifying the players in our school that required manipulation, such as members on the Site-Based Decision-Making Council.

Now here I was the second counselor for him to target. I not only had to deal with the fallout of his professional humiliation but the increased intensity of what he was going to unleash on me as he "doubled down" on his new and improved plan.

Immediately starting at our school, he began the same deceptive tactics of discrediting me like he had done at his previous school. Most of my job duties were taken away. He preyed on the staff that had an empathetic response as he portrayed himself as a "victim" of my incompetency.

His twisting of statements or incidents that involved me were confusing and hard to follow. If I asked questions of him, he would have difficulty regulating his temper and would routinely respond in a loud tirade that would embarrass a normal person. He didn't even notice if there were multiple witnesses or if students had been watching. The next day after his "explosion," I would receive a write-up for my "inappropriate behavior." The reprimand would describe his outburst as if it were mine. There were many of these now piling up in my personnel file suffocating all the favorable performance reviews I had before his arrival.

The personal image the principal projected of himself to others was that he was smart, intelligent, and extremely caring of students; meanwhile, under the radar, his intelligence was that of a "surface skimmer," but his use of language would make it sound like he was extremely knowledgeable about a subject. He had an intense drive for power and control. He was anxious and displayed a nervous pacing pattern at times. He had deficits in problem-solving but was excellent in creating a scenario to deceive others. He could have cared less about the students beyond the means they provided for him to get what he wanted, but he would speak fondly of them if it had a purpose to the listener.

He spent the majority of his day avoiding routine duties as principal and assigned them to others for completion. This made it quite awkward for assignees, as the work was out of their scope and interfered with their normal classroom routine of teaching. It didn't matter to him as he needed to work full-time on his diabolical plan, and those "frivolous" principal duties better not interfere.

Sometimes his anxiety would spiral out of control because my presence was a reminder of the horror he was living. Just my existence within eyeshot erupted vile feelings inside he could not control. That is what someone who is a hater has to live with and you can tell it haunted him. An effective coping mechanism was to leave during the day to meet his "friend" at another school. Our staff never knew he was off-site for frequent extended periods. He even left for a week to attend a professional development course in Colorado and failed to give notice to school staff that he was off campus and out of state. I'm sure his friend counselor probably attended the same conference as well.

Since my whereabouts in the school were highly monitored through the "texting grapevine," nearly all communication in the building was "off-limits" for me. His behavior became very predictable, effective, and gained him enormous power over my every move. There was no place in the school I could go without feeling like I was being stalked.

When I finally realized he had to control every conversation I might be involved in, I used his dysfunction to actually find joy in my miserable day. Every now and then, I would leave my office for no reason and step into a teacher's classroom during planning and begin idle "chitchat" for a few minutes, then wait for him to arrive. I felt like I was teasing a cat with a ball of yarn. It gave me great pleasure knowing I was the one actually controlling his behavior.

Even though I interfered in his daily routine by just existing, it wasn't enough to divert him from the "meat" of his deception, which was to falsely portray student outcomes with manipulated data on test results. He knew I was in the way of his unethical plan, but like most narcissistic people, he believed me "the target" was "really stupid," so he put his deception right out in the open. He figured I was incapable of understanding what they were doing, but it was easy to catch him and several other low-performing teachers at various times taking computerized test for our low-performer students. How ironic! These so-called adults even competed with each other on the scores they achieved. This competition was actually noticeably dumb in their plan because it made the outlier score unbelievable for the targeted student. Because they had such disdain for me, they hadn't even realized I was on the test proctor computer and could see them taking the test for the student who physically was not testing at the time.

Manipulating data required key people to assist him. A school counselor is traditionally very involved with student assessments and various other statistical information.

His plan was to have a counselor who would "look the other way" and allow him to "spoon-feed" false scores into the targeted student's database. This would give the appearance he made a tremendous impact on student achievement, as test scores had risen with the stroke of his falsification. This was unquestionably a genius idea that allowed him immediate recognition and strokes from administration; furthermore, this deceptive ruse played nicely into the projected image he wanted others to believe such as the fact that he must be the "chosen one" to save our low-income school. Their admiration of his ability to turn around a failing school would feed his ego finally with recognition as a "miraculous hero."

Since our school had over a 65 percent staff turnover rate, this created prime conditions for him to slide into a school setting where he could hire most of the staff. As he was familiar with the district, it allowed him to tap "homegrown" resources that he could trust.

This time his plan would be better, more improved, and relentless because now he had developed his team and had all six of them on board. He had methodically hired a group of "washed-up tenured teachers" that had historically been tossed around the district because they could not be fired. As an incentive for their loyalty to him, he placed each on school committees so they could emotionally enjoy power; however, they were ignorant of his underlying motive to control and direct their moves.

The only person standing in his way was me. He was very determined to work hard at implementing his plan to manipulate the Site-Based Decision-Making Council to ensure I was terminated and his "friend" hired. Additionally, to help him with such an important task, he had mentoring from an assistant superintendent who had left our district a few years earlier and was well-known for inflating statistics.

The days had become long, and I truly missed the staff who left, or should I say "escaped," to other schools at the beginning of the year. I had been enduring several boring months of idling without work, being constantly ignored and shut off from communication in everything that was happening in our school; however, one day he unexpectedly appeared in my office. My response to his presence was not what I expected from myself. I felt like a child who had been punished by their parent, and the untamed excitement that rushed my mind was WOW, now he was going to "forgive me." This parent/child feeling came from being broken by him so many times earlier because in every discipline write-up, he always made the statement, "I am your principal and I said so … I don't owe you an explanation for anything!" As much as I hated that juvenile statement every time he used it, somehow it transferred a psychological effect on me that I must admit gave me a glimmer of hope that my punishment might be over now that he has decided to speak to me.

It felt like he was finally acknowledging my existence by stepping into my office. This was rare and gave me an inkling of value. It was like an "awakening" from the blank state of mind I had been previously experiencing. I thought finally "this was it" and that whatever issue he had with me was

OVER, and my delusion made it easy to accept that he truly wanted to work with me.

As we met for a few minutes, his demeanor was charming and very convincing that he was actively engaged in us becoming the principal/counselor team that I had traditionally been accustomed to in my role.

My guard, my gut, and questioning of self was dismissed as I fell for his approach because I had desperately wanted to get to work because I had been idling and idling for a long time and it was pure torture for me. I was miserable having minimal contact with my students, and him finally paying attention to me sparked some much-needed life back into my existence as a counselor. I thought this was the beginning to starting a relationship and putting our school back together. I felt guilty that I had been judging him wrong.

During our meeting, he asked me to outline who the "difficult parents" were in the school. I thought he wanted a heads-up so he wouldn't be blindsided by their behavior, but I also curiously thought, "Why now is he asking me after several months," because most of them had probably flared by now. I was focusing on getting back on track, so ignored my suspicion once again and outlined who they were and the type of behaviors they are known to exhibit.

Surprisingly, within the week after our meeting, I would find that my disclosure of "difficult parents" was to be used against me, as he worked to secure a position for them on the Site-Based Decision-Making Council. He had encouraged the current parents on the council to resign so he could replace them with new parents as representatives so everyone had an "equal chance."

Basically, the appointment of the "difficult parents" meant that this group, who in the past sometimes needed a resource officer to intervene for their aggressive behavior, now had power over whether I kept my position.

This move, allowed the principal to secure more votes for his "friend" by easily reminding the disgruntled parents to direct their anger towards me when they voted for my dismissal, as I was the problem why they had issues with the school in the past.

There were two more positions on the council he needed for complete control of the vote. Both were occupied by dedicated teachers who had been at our school for a long time. This would be a huge undertaking to unseat them from their position.

Not to be discouraged, he forced one who had planned to retire at the end of the year to resign their council position immediately "for the good of the school." He then formulated a more deviant plan to win the other over by nominating her for "Teacher of the Year." In fact, he alone came up with the list of nominees.

In order to guarantee her win, he concocted the idea that all staff members should send their votes directly to him through email. He further assured the school staff that "it was better this way … believe me … and that your vote will be held confidentially!"

Although, many of the staff mumbled that his voting procedure was not appropriate, they reluctantly went along with his request. The other candidates on the ballot were from his gang of washed-out teachers.

This election gave him great joy as he wielded a double-edged sword because he was not only able to handpick "Teacher of the Year" but gave excitement to the other "gang" candidates, a warm fuzzy feeling thinking they were actually nominated by their peers.

By exclusive control of candidate selection and voting, he was not only able to use a prestigious honor to manipulate for his own gain but it allowed the unsuspecting winner to lower her guard on concern he was causing a problem in the school. He was able to diabolically "lure her in" and carefully begin the process of unraveling her previous loyalty to me.

Finally, having the council approve his inexperienced "friend" would provide him a perfect grooming opportunity to develop an administrative partner that would not only be loyal, but most importantly, be willing to "participate" in gaslighting the entire district on how he turned a low- performing school around. This action was a necessary protective layer for him to continue his scam without any accountability. His obsession over her effectively drove him to destroy two schools without conscience in order to get her hired. She was now guaranteed a position by his side that she did not earn.

With the Site-Based Decision Making Council and false test scores securely in place, it was imperative he start on the next tasks, which were to officially remove the non-performing children from intervention services and hide the paper trail tracking students with behavioral issues.

It was an amazing plan in the fact that he didn't have to implement any new programs to move kids around, he just had to have control over the data and everything will fall in place. He ordered me to give security access to his group of followers, and this meant they were able to log in to a student's web-based assessments through their phones and other remote computers in a non-secured testing area of the building. This move removed me from test security, so I had no control over how our testing instruments were implemented and who was taking the test.

I felt this was a conflict of interest for teachers to have unfettered access as it could open the door for testing fraud. Internally, I had wondered why it was so important to open up testing security to so many people, especially non-administrative personnel. This was a huge clue to his plan, and I didn't know what it meant at the time but I certainly needed to pursue where he was headed, especially since this involved the student body.

Luckily, one thing he did not take away from me was access to the student database and my school laptop: this was all I needed to start an investigation to connect the dots on his intertwined scheme.

Every day, all day long since I was basically confined to my office, I secretly started analyzing student data without him interfering. I would compare old test scores with the new, peruse the student's cumulative folder, and look for clues and information about previous testing results and compare report cards. By studying historical assessment results, each student had developed a pattern of growth or non-growth. The students who had a history of increased learning were dropped from further review, as they were on track and had a historical record to match their current scores.

Now something very new was starting to emerge as those who had very minimal growth for years started doing quite well on their assessments. How could this happen? How could a student who showed a certain pattern of academic behavior suddenly break out from norms and start to show phenomenal growth? Was this a miracle, excellent teaching, or just an educational "cocktail" of deceit the new principal had brewed?

He was able to dramatically show rising test results from chronic low-performing students that no other predecessor had accomplished in our school. He miraculously pulled off such a feat in his first three months of principalship. What a rising star he was proving to be!

At dismissal each day during the testing period, the principal would proudly announce the name of students who showed tremendous growth. It was hard to hear each day knowing the results were a lie. Not only did I have knowledge the scores were not true but two other people in the office were well aware.

I can't explain the roaring sound of air leaving the room that occurred when we all looked at each other during the announcements and had great concern that a moral/ethical boundary affecting our students had been deeply crossed by our principal.

He had such joy while calling over the loudspeaker each student's name as they skipped past his office exiting the building to go home for the day. Their parents would be so delighted at how happy their child had become from finally having such academic success.

The two colleagues and I were placed in an ethical dilemma because there is an unwritten rule in the district that you never go over your principal's head. It can be a career-ending decision. So, what do we do with this false information, who do we tell, and most of all, what effect will there be on the student's academic future when they have suddenly lost intervention services in reading and math with one stroke of this false test score?

Essentially, it was becoming clear the non-performing students were easily disposed of, as they were taking up space and using the small amount of funding that was available for their services. There was a distorted belief amongst these incompetent teachers that another, more well-liked child could benefit from the program and possibly produce better test scores. They justified their thinking that the non-performer was simply wasting what little money they had by occupying a space that a more favorable child could benefit from the program.

By removing the non-performer, it would lessen the burden of dealing with the hardship they created for the teacher. This meant the dismissed students who were one to two grade levels behind their peers would have greater difficulty catching up without receiving a modified curriculum.

In order for a student to initially be eligible for intervention services, there needed to be a triangulation of data to collaborate their progress. In the past, there also needed to be this same triangulation to remove them from services. Now, as per the predator's plan, there only needed to be one test score and they could legitimately be removed.

Once a student is released from intervention services, the school must restart the documentation process all over again from the beginning in order for the child to be considered for reentry. It could take up to a year to obtain all the required documentation, meaning a student could possibly add another deficit year behind their peers.

This "unethical restart" not only puts the child at higher risk of academic failure but can greatly impact disengagement from their peer group as educational needs continue to be unmet. Having such a major academic disruption can erode further at their self-esteem and increase thoughts of failure as they struggle in a regular classroom setting that is too far advanced for their level in core subjects.

No student was exempt from harm in his diabolical plan. Not only had some been targeted for academic failure but others had their own personal safety jeopardized as well.

For instance, one day while the principal was visiting his "friend" without notifying staff of his absence, we had a six-year-old boy run away from school and cross a busy four-lane highway. His teacher was one from the "gang." She had mental health issues that should have rendered her incompetent to teach but she was tenured and untouchable.

The secretary tried to keep the boy's disappearance a secret to give the bewildered teacher time to wander around the school looking for him in hopes of finding the child before the news of a missing student leaked from the building.

I was in my office and was finally told of the runaway student when a parent called the school and stated she was driving by and had seen a little boy run down the street. The secretary who took the call reluctantly was forced to tell me about the missing student since someone from the outside now knew. Reluctantly, she was forced to disclose that the principal was off-site again when I asked her to notify him immediately.

I immediately went to look for the child in my car and drove directly to his grandmother's house where he lived. He had run across a major four-lane highway on his journey. Upon my arrival at the home, the grandmother abruptly opened the door and demanded to know "why did his teacher yell at him to go home!" I could not answer her about that statement without incriminating the teacher because it truly sounded like something she would say. All I could think of was thank goodness the little boy was safe in his grandmother's arms.

When a child breaches the school building and leaves the property, there is supposed to be a full investigation and the superintendent is to be notified. When I returned to the school, the principal was still missing.

I immediately started an investigation and asked several people to submit incident statements regarding witnessing the event between child and his teacher. I also asked his immediate teacher to write her version of what happened.

When the principal returned from his liaison with the "friend," he immediately stopped me from obtaining any eyewitness statements from employees and informed me that no further investigation was to take place.

Because there was no internal investigation, this put me in a situation of mandatory reporting when a child is in harm's way. The student is a "flight risk" so I felt that if he ran away again, and something happened to him such as being struck by a car, taken by someone, or harmed in any way, I would be negligent for not reporting the first incident. I had to make an ethical decision to either protect my student or protect the school. I filed a social services report on our school.

The next day, during the social services investigation, they sent a brand-new inexperienced social worker. After she interviewed the teacher, she mentioned to the secretary she was headed to the grandmother's home to obtain her version of what happened.

The school secretary immediately informed the principal, so he headed to the grandmother's home as well. The principal had an urgency to do damage control because at the time of the incident, he was out of the building unauthorized. He also needed to be assured the grandmother was "soothed over" so the incident would not get reported to the superintendent.

I was never interviewed by social services regarding the incident even though I was the one involved in finding the student and filed the report. Later in the week, I saw the social worker walking through our office and inquired about the case I filed. She stated no further action was needed because the teacher had told her that she "didn't know he was going to run away and that it wasn't her fault." "The case is now closed!" the social worker had regurgitated the same verbiage the teacher had said to me after the incident when she called and threatened me not to report the incident.

On the same day of the investigation by the social worker, the after-school director had informed the principal earlier in the morning about the heat and phone lines not working in the building and the temperature was dropping. This happened to be a snow day when we only had ten kids show up for day care.

Later that day, I arrived at the school to pick up papers for my evening class. I checked on the after-school kids as usual. I found them freezing in the gymnasium. It was forty-three degrees and they were shivering. I asked the director if she had reported the issue, and she stated she had asked the principal for portable heaters earlier and he said he would take care of it. This was three hours later when I had arrived and still no heaters were delivered.

I immediately drove to central office down the street to pick heaters up myself, and there was no one in the maintenance department who could help me. I asked the superintendent's secretary to call someone to deliver them as soon as possible to our school. Within minutes of her call, the principal found out I had made the request, so he reprimanded me in writing stating I went over his head and that my behavior was inappropriate.

He had forgotten about the heater situation because that morning he was over at the grandmother's house while the social worker was conducting an investigation regarding the six-year-old who had run away from his teacher.

This incompetent leader, who knows better, was inappropriately interfering with a social worker's investigation and dramatically undermined the seriousness of what happened by manipulating the outcome. This "close call" to him and his incompetent teacher being exposed was first and foremost a priority in "saving his neck" and took precedence over not only the six-year-old runaway but the ten children and school staff who were freezing inside the school building.

The neglect to students continued throughout the school year, as there were many students who came to the office crying and requesting to see me. I was usually at my desk and could hear their distress. It was heartbreaking knowing I was not permitted to provide them service.

The student neglect was rampant, as a number of kids had stopped me in the hallway to say their teacher would not permit them to see me either.

I was building up intense hostility towards him each day at the way our students were being ignored.

Other services we contracted outside the school were starting to notice, as I was privately pulled aside by one of my referral therapists and she asked me why the principal would not allow her to collaborate with me on her cases at our school. She was extremely confused at this policy, as he had informed her that he would be managing the cases instead.

The therapist voiced her concern and noted that traditionally she works directly with the counselor at every school she services. She further stated, "He isn't trained in counseling and cannot offer appropriate help for our combined collaboration. He isn't even meeting the child's emotional needs and reinforcing the treatment plan which was developed specifically by a team."

We had worked together for several years and had excellent collaboration for our shared students up until the arrival of this disrupter.

After the encounter with the therapist, I was informed she was no longer handling our school cases because it would be nonproductive; furthermore, she stated that she would ask her employer to consider terminating the contract with our school or reassign another therapist.

The student neglect continued as I had another therapist from a different agency state that she too was having difficulty connecting with me to discuss our students on her caseload. We had been trying to collaborate especially on a student who had high anxiety.

I had worked with the child a couple times because she happened to come down to the office when the secretary was at lunch and the principal was missing. This was a loophole in their destructive plan that I could take opportunity to see students for a few moments. The bookkeeper usually covered the front desk and was always looking out for kids so didn't hesitate to refer them to me during this rebellion period.

Earlier in the year, I had collaborated with her therapist on anxiety calming strategies and had trained this particular student to help reduce her symptoms. We also worked on problem-solving techniques as directed by her treatment plan. These reinforcers, when needed, played a pivotal role in keeping her anxiety from escalating.

One day as I was stepping out of my office, I noticed this same student standing by the secretary's desk. She was flapping her arms, which was odd and unusual for her but she was smiling. I was standing out of visual sight of the secretary and pointed to myself to silently inquire if the student needed me. She paused and looked at the secretary and then shook her head "no," so I continued on my way.

Thirty minutes later, the bookkeeper approached me with great concern and stated she wanted me to be aware the student was being taken in an ambulance because her anxiety was "over the top," as she was violently shaking.

Apparently, the principal had secretly kept her in his office and did not notify me even knowing I was only ten steps from his office. He wanted to control the situation by placing calls to district nursing staff. The district nurse stated to him she thought it sounded like an anxiety issue based on the described symptoms and referred him to hand the student off to the school counselor. He refused her directions and kept the student hidden in his office, as her anxiety grew more uncontrollable.

When the bookkeeper notified me, I rushed to the hallway and saw my student was being wheeled out on a gurney with several paramedics and the district nurse by her side. I looked the principal straight in the eye as he was passing me in the hallway and asked in a low voice, "Why didn't you let me know she needed me?" He became enraged and shouted very loudly, "This student isn't any concern of yours and you are not to speak to me that way because I am your principal!"

Every person in the office that day who witnessed his response stared at him, and the room became completely silent. I asked him if he could at least go to the hospital with our student. He continued to mumble to himself as he left the building escorting the student on the gurney. The next day, I received another write-up that described his erratic behavior during the incident as if it were mine.

Later during the day of the incident, I heard from the student's teacher that she had been released from the emergency room and the diagnosis was an anxiety attack. Right after that, I received a phone call from the parent and thought it highly unusual that the secretary put the call through to me, but it wasn't long until I found out why. The parent expressed to me how excited she was that the principal was "extremely helpful" with her child's anxiety and he understood that she as a single parent was frustrated at home with her behavior. He also had gone one step further in helping by suggesting that she admit her daughter to an inpatient mental health facility for children and have a full-on psychological evaluation performed. The parent heeded his advice and took her immediately to the inpatient facility after release from the emergency room.

This was an irresponsible overreach from an untrained person who had never collaborated with the outside therapist nor even informed her that the student was being transported to the emergency room; furthermore, it was unfathomable that he felt qualified even further to recommend a psychiatric evaluation to the parent. This child had a therapeutic treatment plan on record with the school that was blatantly ignored by this man.

I was so upset that my student endured such a traumatic chain of events because it was so unnecessary to expose her to that type of serious environment when it could have easily been handled with her therapist and school counselor collaborating together.

In the past, this student had recovered quickly and quite well when reminded of her calming strategies. She would lose minimal class time because of a quick recovery. This was her treatment plan that was on file and, if utilized appropriately and timely, helped tremendously in stabilization which allowed her to reunite with her classmates.

Since her therapist was not notified until a day later, she immediately came to the school very upset in finding out "after the fact" that her student was hospitalized. She asked me why she wasn't notified when the incident occurred so she could meet the child at the hospital. She also wanted to know if I had referenced the treatment plan on file in which we had collaborated. She further stated, "Her client was nowhere near being someone who should be admitted to an inpatient psychiatric hospital!"

Another relationship with an outside agency was now terminated. I could not be trusted to assist this therapist with her clients anymore.

Our school typically had many incidents that required a report to social services. In the past, I was the one who did most of the reporting and was well aware of the background on each case.

I had devised a confidential sign in log book to be placed with the secretary for social workers and therapists to report when they visited a student. It was a separate log from normal visitors to the school. Typically, by the end of the school year, the book would be full of cases, and it served as a beneficial follow-up tool to easily connect with the direct social worker who was handling the case.

This year was definitely different; there were hardly any entries in the book. I would check it periodically and see that not much activity had occurred.

How many reportable incidents and what amount of risk was happening to our students because they were not monitored for abuse or neglect for an entire school year?

Blatantly ignoring student needs affected children with behavioral challenges. Early counseling intervention, development of effective coping strategies, teacher collaboration, working diligently with outside agencies, and parent support were all synergistic cogs that were instrumental for change in helping students achieve equilibrium.

The payoff with having so many caring people involved was enormous for the student when each part cooperated with the other and respected the value of a team. Utilizing a "whole child" approach can be significant in taming a hostile school environment for all children so they could enjoy learning freely. This approach can only work when all individuals connected to the child are practicing the same behavioral plan that was outlined specifically for the student.

Narcissistic staff are disrupters to this process as they feel they have an exclusive relationship with the child and no one else need apply. "Bribery" or "strong arming" are the only tools they know for helping a child stop their unruliness. Until teamwork is centered around the toxic staff's ideology, they will sabotage and undermine any efforts that others may use for intervention so it will not yield a positive result for the student.

During that horrible school year, a lot of our behavior students were unknown to me except through gossip I heard in the work lounge. I didn't have opportunity to build a relationship with most of the students who acted violently, as they were usually hidden in the special education department (SPED) until the end of the school day.

SPED had a lot of equipment for our autistic and disabled students such as specialized swings, computers, mats, handheld therapy devices, etc.

Basically, these were items that would be considered toys for mainstream students, as they were fun and interesting.

Our principal would hide the disruptive child for the day in this department, and they would be entertained by playing freely with any of the equipment. This department was the furthest away from the office and out of sight for most people.

What this meant for our students who were having difficulty in their assigned classroom was their removal tied up SPED staff who now had to supervise them. There was no oversight on how the student was being handled. In other words, did appropriate discipline strategies occur, what happened when the student continued to escalate? Were they restrained and was documentation written?

Most of these students did not have an Individualized Education Plan (IEP) for behavior and legally had no right to have "care" in that department. So, what happened to the students who legally were supposed to receive educational services during the time an unruly student was hidden out?

Unfortunately, the IEP students would not receive mandated services and would have to remain in their regular assigned classroom during the allotted time. Even though there is documentation through daily attendance which noted the student attended school that day, there is no formal record stating they received services according to their IEP as mandated by law. Stakeholders who were not privy to what was going on inside the SPED classroom had no idea students weren't receiving their education for the designated time that was outlined in their IEP.

Behavior students are the most difficult to handle in a school setting. Their disruption can cost valuable education time for not only themselves but their peers who become unwillingly participants when they are forced to stand down and witness their classmate's tirade.

Schools are well aware of the handful of students who are prone to escalate behavior beyond norms and should be able to preplan for an event by training the student and staff in de-escalation skills that benefit restoring the student to acceptable behavior and reuniting them with their peers.

A negligent school culture that is aware of these "high emotional" need students and has failed to address their behavior with a best evidence-based plan as a first measure is susceptible to immediately enforcing "restraint and/or seclusion" as their first line of defense against an unruly child.

Utilizing the latter as a first response is a programmed power struggle that falsely gives the appearance that the teacher and/or school are in complete control of the situation. This false belief is further from the truth.

I have seen a child carried like a football by a supposedly trained professional in applying restraint, and the child had difficulty breathing. I have seen a child who had thrown a pencil at his teacher and immediately put in restraint.

When I saw restraint used on a daily basis in our school, it reminded me of parents who constantly spanked their child. They do such drastic disciplining because they have not yet developed other skills to handle the situation. This unleashing of power over a child is easier to deploy and readily available as a technique to satisfy the immediate needs of the adult to control the situation.

This type of first line usual and customary discipline should not occur in a school setting, especially because it states there are no other options. By becoming routine, this type of handling is susceptible to being "under documented" and dangerous to the student, especially when involved staff look the other way when appropriate intervention guidelines were not followed.

The child can become pre-programmed to know they have the ability to ignite a dysfunctional situation through bad behavior in order to escape doing something they don't wish to do. This manipulation of their teacher works in their favor to regain control over the situation because the reward of being removed from the undesired task is ultimately given.

Our principal and his team were actively engaged in not allowing social learning opportunities for our students. They had no skills in handling difficult behavioral situations but had great strengths in hiding documentation that would reveal safety statistics for our school.

The start of a child's social day, as well as ending, can begin the moment they step on or off the school bus. With so many students on the bus and limited supervision, this is a high-risk environment for behavior to act up. Students can be overstimulated, aroused by other children, or emotionally escalated to lashing out all while the school bus is driving down the road.

Riding the bus can be an important social experience in a child's day that allows them positive engagement with their peers; however, this environment can provide a perfect learning opportunity in the field for addressing social issues when problems arise.

In a toxic school culture such as ours, bus referrals can be hidden from public reporting in the student database in order to boost the reportable safety statistics when reporting to government agencies such as Safe Schools.

When behavioral data is "misplaced," it not only gives a false perception to stakeholders that the school has made great improvements in safety but worst of all, it deprives a student who may have been involved in an altercation from receiving intervention from the school counselor to help them with such an important childhood problem.

A student can be deprived of receiving valuable resources to learn problem-solving, conflict resolution, and compromise. They also are deprived of the perfect opportunity to learn self-awareness from a situation in which they are directly involved and truly understand what transpired.

In one school year, the predator withheld from stakeholders and government reporting agencies over three hundred discipline referrals submitted from multiple bus drivers who complained our students were behaving inappropriately on their way to and from school. Withholding this important data gave the appearance that our principal had improved safety on the school bus when in actuality he made it more dangerous as bus drivers' safety issues were ignored, students weren't accountable for their behavior, and problems carried over into the classroom without counseling intervention.

Depriving a student from a social learning opportunity is a sign of deliberate disrespect to the child. This type of ignoring can easily be found in a toxic school culture where staff minimize the opportunity when presented, have limited skills in dealing with such important childhood issues, and devalue the skills a school counselor can deliver.

In order to pull off the fraud in safety statistics, the principal's "go-to" plan was not only to hide these students out of sight in the special education department but return them to class after they were done playing games on his computer. He knew it was important for parents not to be notified of their child's behavior issue because then it would have to be documented. Some kids would have to remain in his office for hours and were usually given candy as bribes to behave.

The use of candy was a gold standard tool to have kids like him. It was especially effective when the students went home and expressed to their parents how much they liked their new principal. The parents never knew it was because of the volumes of addictive treats he provided. The use of these sweets was multifunctional; he also knew its value during the Kentucky Tell survey on rating our school. He made sure he had control of the classroom where the students were completing the survey. As a principal, it was a conflict for him to even be in the setting because it was about student satisfaction with their school and his presence along with use of candy made it easier for him to manipulate a favorable outcome that would reflect positively on his management of the school.

Personal space was also another constant issue that bothered me as well. He had a student desk in the corner of his office, which meant the child had two walls surrounding them. Often when I walked out of my office, I could see him through the door window towering over a student and his body within inches from their face. Because they were seated, they were trapped with his private area basically on top of them. They had no way to get away. Most of the time this was happening was when he was extremely mad at the student and wanted to display power to control them, but some kids would fight back, kick, and yell at him to "get away." Others who were more compliant were able to enjoy sitting on his lap and playing computer games with him.

Even a fundraiser felt disturbing when he announced an event for a new playground, which I thought odd because ours was only five years old and was in very good shape. He devised a way to make fast money, and that was to charge fifty cents for each student who wanted to duct tape him to the wall of the gymnasium and for a dollar they could smash a pie of whip cream in his face.

The whole incident looked like something out of the show *Dexter*, as he had a plastic trash bag over his clothing for pie throws but the lower part of his body was duct-taped to the wall. Kids who did the duct-taping were at the same height as his private area, and he had duct tape all over it fastening him to the wall.

When I walked into the gymnasium to see how the fundraiser was going, I was shocked at the whole situation. I looked at a teacher standing next to me and stated, "Am I the only one bothered by this?" There were many adults looking on, and I felt that as long as he was doing this out in the open, the adults were able to dismiss their own thoughts that it was inappropriate. Was this a "group think" type of situation that if no one were brave enough to say it was inappropriate, then his actions were acceptable? The teacher had no reaction. Maybe I was just being biased because I was suspicious of everything he did, so I left immediately.

Later that day after the fundraiser, I had two girls that were sent to me for "counseling" because they were caught by the teacher passing a note back and forth which stated "the principal has big privates!" The teacher did not want the principal to know about the note because she was embarrassed, so she referred them to me.

I have no idea if he had sexual predatory intent. All I know is this predator had a plan, and it wasn't good for our students.

CHAPTER 08:

THE PREDATOR'S PROTECTOR

Since there are no laws to protect employees or students from becoming a target of a hate assault unless they are in a protected group, then at the very minimum, the superintendent of the school district should ethically be willing to at least investigate an egregious allegation that has been launched under their leadership.

The lack of inaction or willingness to ignore an alleged accusation places the protector as a willing participant. There are many reasons for taking this avenue, which may include arrogance, allegiance, inexperience in role, like-mindedness as the predator, or inability to be effectively objective.

When a supervisor at a high level lacks the capacity to understand that clinically significant personality disorders may exist inside their company and can be extremely disruptive to the operations, they are uneducated and place the organization at risk of unethical destruction.

A supervisor protector who lacks insight to investigate and shield from harm those under their realm places themselves on an even parallel as the predator they protect. They are an accomplice in abusive behavior and should be equally accountable for harm caused by their inaction.

A superintendent who protects a predator and grossly allows such toxic behavior to exist can easily cover up the problem due to lack of oversight.

They also enjoy the availability and easy access to the district's legal team of lawyers who are on contract.

When it becomes more important for a superintendent to cover up a problem within legal boundaries, in order to release the district of liability, than it is to deal with the magnitude and scope that an abusive impropriety has on their students and employees, they are not only unskilled in problem-solving and critical thinking but do not belong in such a powerful position, especially when it involves the welfare of children.

The disengaged superintendent surrenders to accepting that children and staff can be broken as long as it is not illegal. Because they lack the ability to completely understand the full impact of their decision-making, they are unable to comprehend their role in the development of long-term mental health issues on staff and student targets whom they did not protect.

To further complicate the issue with my boss, our superintendent was a member of the same union that represents employees, and I felt this was a conflict of interest for fairness and objectiveness when I had consulted with my union rep as an employee. The handling and familiarity with the union on other cases within the district has an impact on the union relationship between the two organizations. It was impossible for me to have my case heard objectively when I was placed at such a disadvantage of being outnumbered in representation.

If the union does not recuse themselves from representing the superintendent when they are involved in allegations, the toxicity in the district will continue as allegiance of the union is biased towards the superintendent.

The human resources department easily can become a willing participant in allowing toxic dysfunction to exist within its labor force because more than likely they are not trained in recognizing clinically significant pathological behavior in its employees. This makes them highly vulnerable to be manipulated by predatory staff.

This lack of education and training easily allows the HR decision-maker to side with the predator since they have already been "covertly groomed" in believing an employee or witness is a "difficult person" prior to an actual complaint. This "grooming" is an effective tool for a predator to block an employee from transferring to another location within the organization or have validation on their grievance.

A toxic district further allows the disruption to erode a school deeper because it fails to implement standards and policies for a target or witnesses to come forward and be protected from retaliation or job loss.

Why did our superintendent recommend the predator to our Site-Based Decision-Making Council? He already showed previously in our district he wasn't capable of running a school, and that is why he left in the middle of his contract. What allegiance did she have to him?

Because our superintendent utilized a faulty business model that lacked investment in its staff, she would engage in mass hiring and disposing practices. This dysfunctional tradition made it easier for leadership to forego mentoring employees and easily overlook untapped talent. Problem employees could be tossed to the unemployment line and high-risk low-income schools could remain in a constant state of rebuilding as disgruntled tenured employees are assigned to these types of schools. This faulty business model made it appear the district was addressing the needs of the school through new programs that were just actually recycled and repackaged nonproductive ideas from earlier failures.

The predator had left our district several years earlier under unfriendly circumstances. What made him different now and how did the superintendent come to change her mind? Did her dysfunctional hiring model and routine termination practices falsely give her the impression that previously disposed of employees were now better after they went away for a while and then returned? Did she lie to herself in thinking that having a lack of investment in the workforce would be the gold standard for quality employees?

Something I could not understand was why the superintendent was willing to cover up for the predator's misgivings yet strike the iron hard on me. I think it was because she was weak, and I was even weaker so that was the easier road to travel.

CHAPTER 09:
FIGHT BACK OR SURRENDER

One of the most complicated decisions I had to make was whether to fight back, confront, or submit to my predatory boss. I wrestled for a long time trying to figure out the best approach but became paralyzed when considering any of the options because none of them would save me from a catastrophic consequence.

There was not one single angle or approach that would wholly express my concerns and explain my story to someone who could help me find a solution. I was outnumbered, and this problem of pathology I was forced to deal with was very much outside my scope of complete understanding.

This inability to express and comprehend my situation was the barrier to not seeking counseling for myself as well. I just didn't know how to state my situation, and what if I had a counselor who was not experienced in helping targets of predatory behavior?

I did not have the energy to fail again or "enlighten or explain" what was happening because every day there was one incident after another stacking up. There was no way to process the meaning of one event because another was right behind to mask the meaning of the first.

There are no words that can be said in a summary to explain what was happening, and furthermore there was no one with administrative oversight that would be interested in what I had to say.

For survival, it was just easier to decide which incidents really matter more than the others. I had to reason with myself every day: "Oh, that one wasn't too bad or I didn't like it but who cares it's really minor in comparison to other thing that happened." I guess measuring the incidents on a scale of 1 to 10 allowed me to discard some so they wouldn't keep stacking up so fast.

It took every bit of energy for me to come to work each day. When I walked into the school every morning, my heart was heavy, my brain had layers of fog, and I would feel rudderless in direction. I had lost the ability to even smile, and everywhere I looked I saw immeasurable pain. I felt I was the loneliest person in a populated area that was sprawling with activity.

All the joy I had known working in an elementary school was no longer accessible to me even though I could see and hear my students. I was amongst a sea of clients who didn't understand that I was suffering profoundly at the loss of helping them and knew some would never complete high school because of a few toxic people who had made that decision on their behalf. It was as if I were on a lifeboat with many provisions and I was watching my students drown while I did nothing.

I knew I couldn't confront my predatory boss because there was an extreme power differential between us and he had the security of the superintendent to back up any decisions he made. I had already tested him with several challenges that ignited explosive tantrums which resulted in me being written up for his behavior.

I had a cautious desire to go on the offensive since I had spent all my reactions in defending myself. Internally, I played with the idea of attacking him in the school community through emails by calling out everything he was doing, but that would have looked petty on my part and it was too late. I should have sunk my ship earlier before he had time to propagandize to others about my incompetence.

I also could have reacted with a schoolwide email welcoming his counselor "friend" by name as our new school counselor for next year. I just kept her name to myself but knew if I had exposed her identity, there may have been a sliver of hope he wouldn't have secured approval of her to take my position. This was actually my best choice, and I didn't have the guts to go through with it.

It actually was an excellent idea that I contemplated. It would have been genius on my part because I would have created a double-edged sword for a final coup de grace on the predator. By mentioning her name before I was actually terminated would have made it impossible for him to hire his pick because the narcissism in him would have to admit I was right. On the other edge of the sword, the superintendent would not have allowed him to hire her because he would have violated labor policies of selecting someone before the job is posted and interviews have taken place.

I kept thinking about how two schools had been destroyed because of this dynamic duo. I wanted the destruction to stop but that is like asking someone with pathological tendencies to be cured of their ailment overnight. They would just destroy another school again.

This predator felt entitled to steal what I had earned. He also believed it was okay to rob our students of their future because no one will ever find out. He had built an indestructible network of power and securely manipulated protection. He had the comfort of delivering a legal assault on the students and me without accountability and furthermore had a cult following of weak people to advocate for his greatness. It would take years to purge the evildoers from our school, as tenure can guarantee they can enjoy a life of delivering hatred.

I felt surrendering was like quitting. That was uncomfortable for me and not familiar. I don't quit! I was abandoning my students and breaking bond with 413 students, and that was deeply devastating to me.

CHAPTER 10:
FRIENDS SCATTER

Trust is such a sacred state of being. It's a feeling that positively contributes to emotional security when you are confident in sharing a friendship with others. Personally, I was driven towards seeking individuals that mutually honored our existence as human beings, respected our differences, and had the desire to grow as comrades by supporting one another through conversation, action, and loyalty.

When one of us failed, we both experienced the pain, and when one of us succeeded, we both shared in the accomplishment. It should be a relationship without harm, jealousy, or malice. It should be unconditional and equal.

What I didn't factor was the intense on-the-job learning of sociopathic behavior that came as a result of being a target. This exposure way outpaced the knowledge and experience my friends understood, so manipulation and undermining of our friendship was easily achieved by the predator as part of his overall plan.

He lurked through the school determined to seek my connected relationships and covertly manipulate turning the alliances upside down. My allies did not understand the undermining in which he was delivering to destroy our friendship. It didn't make sense; it was smooth and convincing one deceit at a time.

Most individuals have not experienced being a target of a predatory boss. Most everyone has experienced a "jerk" boss at one time or another, but this does not compare to dealing with a sociopathic person who lacks an empathetic response and is well prepared to deliver a planned execution on a target.

Friends, who were once loyal, can lack the ability to grasp and understand the impact of predatory behavior nor do they want to be a part of its destruction, so the only way to make sense of a very bad situation is self-preservation.

How can they make sure the predator doesn't come after them? As sorrowful as they empathize with me, they knew in their heart the friendship must detach in order to preserve their own career and maintain status in the school because he has power over them too as their boss.

Because these friends viewed our separation with no malice, they expected I would understand. There was no consideration for the emotional effects of the loss.

My friends did lend a sympathetic ear, but they projected to me I should be able to handle the situation on my own because they had confidence in my abilities. Unfortunately, I was not looking to fight a battle by myself because this was an all-out war not only against me but most importantly our students as well. This virus in our school was something that needed everyone to come to the battlefield but no one wanted to take the risk.

Factors that contribute to witness action or inaction can include their own implicit bias with regards to who has the majority on their side, who controls the power, how will I be affected?

This consideration for self is invaluable for decision-making. They will often opt for a more favorable solution by accepting moral disengagement to fix their dilemma. This can easily be achieved by distancing themselves from the unethical behavior because "others have not come forward."

The predator in our school bounced quickly from deception to deception, which gave the appearance of what he was doing seem too complicated to follow. This illusion worked to his benefit because most weren't able to process the consequences of the prior act before another one appeared. This "slippery slope effect" gave a perception that nothing of monumental value was really happening because the "piecemealing" of the assault diluted its effects to others. It took too much emotional energy for understanding the full picture, so witnesses would accept minimizing the reality to remain disconnected.

A witness did not ask to be part of a predatory plan nor did they ask to be a protector of the target. They have been abruptly put in a "lose-lose" situation by merely being in the wrong place at the wrong time. Being forced to address an issue that involves ethics or morals from a situation they did not ask creates a personal dilemma that becomes overwhelming.

A protective decision is necessary through disengaging which will help alleviate that unsettling feeling of knowing something is wrong, but they don't have the capacity to solve the problem.

A witness will weigh the risk associated with coming forward and realize more than likely it would not alleviate their emotional turmoil but could place them in harm's way for their present employment. This overriding fear is why witnesses stay silent because most companies, especially schools, do not have an independent safe place to report inappropriate behavior especially against students by one of their colleagues. This is a risk that outweighs a benefit.

I knew my friends were on the fence between supporting me or keeping their livelihood. Protecting their own job was vitally necessary for their own survival, especially in a small town where rumors could ruin you, so they began distancing themselves for protection. It was imperative the predator would not sense their support or think there was an alliance with me.

Since I had limited access to students, I had been "sideways" contributing through the team, and now this avenue was completely gone. It was clear to me I had lost being part of the cooperative effort and was no longer accepted in my school community.

I deeply felt the disconnect from my support system as ultimate betrayal and hated the way evil was rewarded when I witnessed the predator merrily going about life with no accountability.

Years of friendships were rapidly wiped from my existence making me feel if they were ever real in the first place. I also viewed the rejection as a "backhanded slap" to our students because these same people claimed the children were why they enjoyed teaching.

The students and I had become bundled in a group and labeled "throwaways" as our history with the school community was wiped from memory and a new false narrative was put in motion. The separation from my friends was interpreted in my mind as aligning with the predator even though they may have thought differently in their decision-making.

This loss put me in a cycle of repetitive negative thoughts about my coworkers and why they suddenly dropped their goal to speak up for children and aligned with the predator's unethical behavior. This was such hypocrisy and radiated even more questioning of the perceptions I had formed from our many years together. It fueled intense anger inside me not only at them but myself as well for forming such a false belief in trusting our friendship as real.

Unfortunately, what I hadn't realized at the time was my team was not as privy to all the deception the predator was designing and I had wrongly assumed they were in the know. Maybe if I had given it more insight during the battle, I would not have felt so brokenhearted for such a long time when they left me behind.

The loss of my friends was a deep pain that was quite overwhelming and had me reflect back on the many counseling sessions I had with retained students who discussed the loss of their friend group. I had the same feelings they faced when forced to stay behind because a child who has been retained will never forget that traumatic event for the rest of their life nor can the adult who suffered the consequences of targeted destruction of their work life.

Our retained students continued to have the burden of seeing their former classmates each day as they walked throughout the school. These daily sightings had to be a constant reminder that reinforced they were not a part of something because every retained student I worked with brought up the traumatic experience of losing their friend group even if years had passed since retention.

People who don't understand the grief of a sudden disconnect from a peer group will unfortunately make remarks such as "you will make new friends" or in my case "you will find another counseling position easy." These words are not comforting at all because it never acknowledges or validates the pain of losing so many friends at once, especially since it wasn't my choice nor my students' when they were retained.

CHAPTER 11:
FORMING A PLAN TO KILL THE PREDATOR

Warning: this part of my memoir is very graphic. I wanted to document the power of my internal thoughts that rapidly developed in an opportune moment. This was an impromptu idea that gave me permission to justify revenge against a predator who had wielded unyielding power over me and the students. The reprehensible manner of my projected idea during this weakness felt extremely real and vivid. The constant daily harassment and hatred inflicted on me and my students by my supervisor had been building up to a breaking point. This incident gave me direct insight into how workplace violence can insanely become justified in an instant.

It was beginning to come clear I would be forced to accept the fate of what he planned for me. I had come to feel like a cornered animal, thinking my only way out was a violent attack against the monster who purposely destroyed my existence in the world I had known.

A sudden urge to kill the predator came to me during a specific opportunity. It wasn't something I had ever thought of before because that is not who I am. I didn't believe anyone should ever take another's life, but I had been pushed to a hopeless breaking point from his relentless attacks that had invaded my entire existence as a person and professional.

He had succeeded in dramatically digging into the depths of my worldview where I had not gone before. This unlocking opened my mind to view that some people are not really attached to life and they could care less if they harmed another human being even if it's a child. I had come to deeply believe he was a predator.

It happened on a weekend, I was driving from my cousin's house and was doing my usual cut through the neighborhood by the school. That was my ordinary route for years, and each time, I would glance over at the building and make sure everything looked okay.

On this routine passing, it became like no other. I would be stopped in my tracks, as there was a vehicle parked near the front of the school. It appeared to be a lone visitor. I could clearly see it was the predator's truck.

Why was he at the school by himself? I thought. During the regular school day, it was a normal sighting for him to have a loyal minion by his side he was rarely alone.

I pictured him inside the school "sharpening his talons" and stroking a "trophy of power" that he made for himself. It was odd to think he was alone but he probably didn't want his followers to see a certain part of his plan, so I justified that is why he was there on the weekend. The empty building gave him unchecked access to feeding his paranoia. He could easily sift through classrooms and check on his monitoring devices without detection.

I wanted him to be alone and kept noting that it was only his vehicle in the parking lot. I had perused the entire school ground and no other cars were on the property. I determined and confirmed in my mind he was alone and sat there with my car idling.

Intrusive thoughts flooded my head on how easy it would be for me to quietly sneak in the backdoor of the school and easily kill him with a gun.

The construct of each move I would need to make ran so vividly through my head that even the turning of the key to penetrate the door seemed so easy. I knew in my mind once I crossed the threshold, I was committed to the act so there would be no looking back.

The street where I was idling was not traveled very much. I kept checking my mirrors and scanning all around to see if any witnesses would interfere. There was no one, and I felt the opportunity to wipe him out was given to me. I could do it, and no one would know until the next day.

The feeling of power enveloped my being as I played the act in my head. I was very calm in my delirium and felt justified that he needed to not be of this earth anymore. He was evil that would never know consequences, so I could easily deliver a final assault because he had stolen my existence from earth anyway.

Thinking of my students, I felt like a mother who had to protect her kids from harm because no one else had authority or courage to come forward. He had done enough damage in such a short time and needed to be stopped. I felt his wrath would never end for our students even long after I was gone. I thought of how many future kids would be affected by his actions, as he would be able to rise further in his deception with the protection of the new school counselor he had hand-groomed after my firing.

Killing him instantly with a gun was too good for him. A gun was not what I wanted to use after thinking about it for a moment. It was important to me that he suffer slowly and painfully like I did each and every day I went to work. I wanted him to die a slow and torturous death that would have him begging for his life like a crying coward. His voice would become pitched like that of a little boy as he expressed his broken childhood. He would continue to utter that his actions were never personal but defend hate as easier to deal with since he too was a victim.

I viewed him not only as a predator in the sense of his actions to destroy people but I also felt he had been sexually abused as a child. Even though I have no knowledge of his past, I had witnessed many coincidences of "grooming" or "questionable" behavior with our students.

As I continued idling in the street, I envisioned having him lying on his desk wrapped tightly with cellophane so he could not move. He had too many covert acts with children that involved touching in a planned way. I wanted to mimic his *Dexter* role like he did when the students had duct-taped him to the wall for a playground fundraiser. I wanted to call him out on his own behavior and that it will be duplicated on him. He will come to understand that I will control his outcome.

It was important for his office to be the crime scene because he had so grossly contaminated its sacred function. As he lay there bound, I would deliver a daunting reminder he was going to die as punishment for stealing the emotional health of so many children and sending them on a perma-nent path of failure. There would be a sharp instrument in my hand to taunt across his eyes to arouse fear. As I slowly walked around his pathetic body to arrive at my final destination, I would deliver with intense anger a blunt forced puncture to the area he liked to put in children's faces. This disabling action also served for him to feel intense pain. His cowardice cries would be ignored as I stand there callously like he was to me and the students he victimized.

In the aftermath, I could easily leave the predator to his own demise, as I felt my power had been reclaimed. He became nothing to me and hope-fully the final act had cleansed the poison from his body. He is trash, and they will discard of him in the morning as his humiliated body will tell his story when the superintendent is called to cover up another mess.

My delusion seemed to last forever without interruption as my imagination deeply walked through the details of "killing him off." I was concerned at how fast and easy a plan had come together. It was such a graphic detailed vision that felt so real and doable. This scheme had never entered my mind until this opportune moment. I am very concerned and shamed by this evil beast that now emerged inside me.

I had envisioned a vivid murderous rampage that seemed quite controlled to me. Thankfully, my ability to self-regulate and plan beyond the impulse allowed me to comprehend that I had no right to kill him no matter how right it felt at the time.

Later on, after days passed and real life continued, it was quite difficult to fade these corrupt feelings from entering my mind because of the continued daily exposure of the hostile work environment.

I knew if I didn't wrangle these horrible thoughts, I would become just like him, so I worked towards rewriting the violent narrative and tried to replace it with a more humane way of justice.

By imagining his future in my own narrative and accepting, whether it truly happened or not, was the answer to having control over my own resolve.

This rewrite would require my ability to be patient once again, as I chose to wait for "natural consequences" to eventually catch up with him.

I could see his marriage falling apart when his wife realizes how unethical, and immoral he was in choosing to fight for another woman. She would be further horrified with the realization that he had committed crimes against children especially since they shared two of their own together.

His church would no longer see him as the upstanding Christian he claims to be each Sunday, and their shunning would remove him from a community in which he had enjoyed immense recognition. Finally, I pray his unmasking would permanently remove him from a school career where he could no longer contribute to the toxicity of more schools and affect the outcome of children's lives.

I see his followers fade in disgrace and recognize they need to retire from ever being employed in a school setting.

Finally, the protector superintendent who allowed all this to happen in her district will have full knowledge of what her ignorance did to the very students under her care as their parents file lawsuits. Employees who were witnesses would no longer fear for their own career, as policies and laws were enacted to protect them.

Unfortunately, long after my firing, natural consequences did not have time to prevail, as the predator was rewarded, like all incompetent people who bully their way to the top; he was awarded a promotion to assistant superintendent in a nearby county. He left our school one year after his predatory plan was enacted. He destroyed two elementary schools, and it will take many years to "weed out" all the like-minded teachers he left behind.

As for the superintendent, she retired a year after the predator safely moved into his new promotion. Her legacy should never be repeated, and no other public-school child should ever have to experience hatred of this type from adults in their school environment again.

CHAPTER 12:
THE URGE TO HARM

The protective factors that changed my decision to not kill the predator were not effective on suppressing the urge to harm him. He was most unfit in the education field. In fact, he was a person who should never occupy a powerful position in any company. Because he cannot control his own behavior or impulses, he required direct supervision from an administrator who would demand accountability for his acts. None of this was in play at our school district, so our students went unprotected.

The predator had violated the "sacred space" of a child's learning environment. Someone had to stand up and call him out but that couldn't happen because he was the boss and there was a powerful protector guarding him.

It felt like the doors of justice had been slammed in my face and were forcing me to just sit back and let it happen. I felt constant seething and anxiety knowing we would not be rescued. The unjustness of the situation left me with a heavy burden of finding my own way to liberation. With it came the compounding responsibility of figuring out how to bring 413 students along.

His actions had violated trust in the education system, and no one who had power over him was willing to excise his cancerous virus from spreading in our school. I had experienced an extreme emotional assault from this evil person and was rendered emotionally spent. Because of his maltreatment and clever ability to get away with it, I had become educated in a way my brain had never perceived.

Witnessing these pernicious acts awakened my psychological ignorance to finally understand how someone like the predator can easily be a chameleon in a school setting, especially with a protector who allowed him to continue his diabolical reign of terror without accountability.

While resiliency had positively moved me forward through life in times of trouble, I had unknowingly buried the effects of some traumas because I survived and nothing else mattered at the time.

During childhood, I endured eighteen years living with a brother who was physically and emotionally abusive, then I married and survived twenty more years with a spouse who disrespected me almost the same way. Now it was happening again, but this time evil had come to my workspace and deeply lacerated through the calluses that had protected me from my previous pain. I had falsely believed that I would never be in an emotionally injurious situation again because I had been careful.

My brother, my spouse, and my boss were all situations in which I felt no control. Being everyone's target had become my emotional history. You see predatory people enter your space freely. They are allowed access because they cannot be reasoned with, as their worldview is so vastly different and complicated yet simple. To survive them is to take away your belief system and norms that made you. I began to question why I was so different.

These "freeloaders" roam through life without conscience while I tried to live by mine. We were unmatched people in strength, and the ability to emotionally feel was my downfall that churned desires of lashing out.

My urge to harm was brewing at the predator's "followers" as well. I knew they were nobody without the direction of their false idol. His followers were mere minions that were weak burnt-out teachers that had lost their self-respect by their own doings throughout their career.

They were individuals who were easily manipulated by him and had no idea that in a moment he could easily take away membership in his club when he rendered them no longer useful. This breakup would emotionally destroy their already fragile psyche.

I had such mixed emotions for witnesses who refused to come forward and advocate for our students. Most were my friends, and now I could only think of them as cowards. I resented how they easily looked the other way and continued enjoying the security of their job.

Dealing with the predator, protector, followers, and witnesses every single day continually fueled my anger to harm in some way. Maybe not in the physical way but emotionally if only they could have the same thing happen to them, it would help me feel better maybe.

As a professional school counselor, I had failed in my advocacy for the 413 students. I was frustrated, sad, angry, and lacked skills to combat a predator and his team, so the urge to harm continuously fueled inside my being. Grief would eventually have to become my antidote to settle these harmful urges for good.

CHAPTER 13:
MISGUIDED PASSION

After my scheduled "firing," I had time to reflect on my profession as a school counselor, particularly why it was extremely difficult to leave the dead-end predicament I had found myself completely imprisoned.

Deep inside it was passion that deflected me from seeing the light. We all have it inside us that drives towards one thing or another, and it is what guided me into having a high desire to make a positive impact on children. I did not want to give up a position that made such a difference in the lives of children and was so personally rewarding.

I had put a lot of effort and sacrifice into obtaining my career choice, so like most, I worked hard towards an upper-level degree in the specialized field and then fully dove into the profession after I had finally secured a position. I fell in love with my career choice and felt extreme passion when providing counseling and saw the difference my services provided for my students. Their feedback was extremely rewarding and reinforced that I made the correct decision to become a school counselor.

Anyone who knew me professionally would say that counseling is what I was meant to do in life. It seemed to be my calling but now I had been forced into a power struggle with the predator to defend my passion, and when he ultimately won, I began to question every part of who I was.

His win had drawn me to a more perfect understanding of the power that passion had on my life. It became clear I had put all my eggs in one basket not even thinking about the wolf lurking outside to gobble them up.

This extreme encounter in my work life came completely out of nowhere. I had been so busy driving forward that I was blindsided by a massive obstacle that T-boned my existence and would become life-changing. Normally one person shouldn't change your direction but when you add immense power to endorse their attack, they have security and I have fear. They will never feel fear and I will never feel security in that type of environment again.

The predator had unmasked a malignant virus that plagued our school which seemed to have been tradition for a very long time.

In the aftermath, this revelation helped me understand I could no longer fight from inside the school because I was way outnumbered and my emotional health had reached critical status. I would have to figure a way to speak for my students from the outside, and that is why I wrote this journal.

I had lost passion in ever returning to work as a school counselor not because I didn't enjoy the field but because I no longer believed in the education system itself. I felt it had drifted far away from truly respecting the needs of children especially when it comes to mental health. I was massively bothered by the fact that so many corrupt people didn't even blink an eye when they falsified test scores or bullied children and easily separated them from their peer group. I wondered how systemic this problem was in all the public schools in the United States.

Our district lost its passion years ago when it packed administration with nepotism and secured key positions for friends regardless of qualifications. What a circle of protection they all enjoyed along with some of the highest paying positions in the district. The teacher's union also relished in their share of corruption by internally infiltrating our district, as they had employees who had a position on the school board. Yep, no conflicts of interest that couldn't be managed as all angles were covered to protect the elites. This made it easy to pay attention to the loudest adults up front, and that is the center of a toxic school district's business model.

With all these protective layers of bureaucracy in a public school, it is my opinion that the business model for delivering education considers adults first and at the very bottom of what's left over are "just good enough" investments for the students.

We all expect children to succeed and will proudly use those words in a slogan, but in reality, we really don't act like that's our mission. This inversion is why low-performing schools will remain constant and why non-performing children are high-risk for becoming targets by adults or experience disengagement from their peers. This is why talent can't stay and this is why some students will wander away from their academic community never realizing their full potential. These are the reasons I have lost my passion for a position I once loved. My passion had blinded me to the true reality of what was going on in our schools and sadly had been just a snapshot in time that I will truly relish but know I can never return to that feeling again.

The predator had passion too; unfortunately, his drive was for helping himself no matter what means were involved. Ironically, passion can be a destroyer or it can be a positive motivator, but I know one thing for certain, predators do not have the right to steal passion from children, and a school district should know that children are not born for the purpose of a predator's pleasure.

When I was growing up, I lived a nightmare life with a brother who had massive anger issues. It was pure hell and the school for me was my safe space where I could not be harmed, enjoyed learning, and had great success through my academic efforts.

I don't know where I would have ended up had my school not provided me with such an enriched environment where teachers were wholly invested in student outcomes.

My school fostered purpose and hope which had led me to a passion for learning.

After my encounter with the predator, it seems passion should never be permanent but it should be evolving into unknown areas that I would have never considered before, had I not been shoved out of my existing passion, and maybe that's not a bad thing.

CHAPTER 14:
WORLDVIEW

We all have an internal worldview that guides us through life and hopefully was nurtured with positive experiences while forming so we can mostly enjoy a lifetime in equilibrium.

Some individuals such as children unfortunately are not able to experience life balance when their worldview is developing. A drastic negative trauma that disturbs homeostasis can change the trajectory of one's life as they struggle to process unsettling feelings and question purpose.

Encountering the predator, especially in a sacred environment such as a school setting, was not only shocking but a tragedy that he would carelessly impact a child's future without remorse.

He had the ability to draw me into his evil world and alter my worldview with precision pruning like that of a powerful surgeon. Equally, I can only imagine the horrible effect on the students and the magnitude of their failures knowing the root cause will never be traced back to him.

I didn't like the fact that my mind went to such a deep dark place and opened me to areas of thinking I would have never considered before. This darkness overshadowed my wellness with utmost disrespect and became a leading role in my life for the time being. Eventually, I could only sever its grip after I gained the ability to understand its function.

The predator hadn't physically abused me, which would have been actually easier to escape in the beginning, since I would have legal protection from the assault. He could be brought to justice and hopefully face accountability for his behavior through severe judicial consequences. My story would definitely have a different outcome and probably no students would have been harmed. I more than likely would still be enjoying my counseling position today and serving the 413 children who needed my help.

Because it was emotional professional abuse driven by hatred, I had to bear the entire burden privately and accept the consequences for being a target. Having such an unprovoked attack directly on my existence was shattering and left me wondering where do I go from here?

I often wondered about the effects on my students and how having test scores altered, intervention services taken away, and denied access to counseling would change their worldview when feelings of failure, disconnect, and hopelessness began to erode their purpose in life. My students were innocent bystanders that were developing children. How dare a few individuals feel they have the power to alter the course of their young lives by simply tossing them away.

I had worked with several children who had oppositional defiant disorder (ODD), and a common theme at the basis of their defiance was not being believed by an adult. They received no validation for their story, so when the adult in their life continually reinforces their belief as not true, the child will begin to lose trust. They understand there is a liar in the house and they have no way to make it right. This creates an unsettling worldview change that nothing matters anymore, so they engage towards aggressive behaviors because their words didn't work.

School staff are equally influential as caregivers to a child and can easily affect a negative outcome from continual toxicity they place on the student.

A child knows when a teacher or other school staff are lying. They also know when adults have given up and no longer advocate for them.

Although a student won't be able to pinpoint what happened during their school career by predatory school staff, I believe they will develop internal feelings of disconnect from the school community as time goes on because academics increasingly become more difficult. An enormous psychological imbalance will also occur through the loss of their peer group when classmates move ahead.

I believe that incompetent school staff who hate a particular student can increase the chance that a child's worldview can be altered in a negative fashion due to relentless toxic encounters, especially if it singles out the child from their peer group. How can we help school districts understand the seriousness of changing a child's precious worldview through this type of toxic exposure?

I was an adult with many graduate courses in counseling and having my worldview violated with evil was extremely difficult to understand. I became centered around doubt, mistrust, and anxiety with more symptoms to come as the assault penetrated deeper into my belief system. I was in a permanent state of flight and desperately needed to find a secure place to be that others could not understand. This negative worldview transition was instrumental in putting me on a path of violent thinking, depression, and suicidal ideation.

As a target, I had repetitive overwhelming thoughts of "you might as well kill me … I'm already dead." I can't even imagine the thoughts my students felt when their worldview was drastically changed by hatred in their school community.

CHAPTER 15:
MINUTES BEFORE SANDY HOOK

This part of my memoir was personally transforming for me as a counselor earlier in my career. My perspective of the students I counseled was elevated after this tragedy, as I wanted answers beyond the violence. Stepping back, I evaluated from a macro perspective and it became clear to me that we were undervaluing the significance of children's mental health in their school community.

This is my account on that horrific day as we were coincidently conducting a mandatory active shooter drill within minutes of the actual Sandy Hook tragedy.

My job was to clear the second floor and make sure every classroom was following the procedure to keep students safe. It appeared as if the routine inspection would go smoothly as planned. I checked doors, made sure there were no kids in the hallway, and that all windows leading into the classroom were covered.

On the final leg of my inspection, it appeared a door was still open. This homeroom belonged to one of our first-year teachers.

I stopped outside the entrance and noticed he was hurriedly thumbing through a metal ring that appeared to have over twenty-five keys. I could tell he was having difficulty differentiating the door key, as they all looked the same. Of course, it disturbed me that he wasn't prepared, especially knowing ahead of time that we had scheduled the drill. I thought to myself this is exactly why we practice.

During active shooter preparation, I have always been positioned on the outside hallway and have never actually been inside a classroom to see how students react. While I was waiting for the teacher to find his key, I decided to step into the classroom in order to have an idea how the kids were responding.

As I glanced around the corner, I was shocked at what I saw. A large human huddle of twenty-six students was formed. They had their arms draped around each other securing one another for safety.

There was one child I could see on the outside of the huddle who appeared to be an outlier. He was in tight with the group but standing upright instead of bent over like the others. He stared at me intensely with his piercing blue eyes. He didn't say a word but his presence was powerful as we stood there staring at one another for a brief moment. It was obvious he was fearful about the drill, and I too felt an overwhelming sense that our procedures were wrong.

His position on the outside was the most vulnerable to an active shooter. I felt he realized this, and his compliance with teacher placement was conflicting with his mind to save himself. He was a good student and never gave his teacher any problems nor questioned his authority. There had to be a message here but I didn't know what it was without deeper understanding.

In schools, we are notorious for reacting and doing things that make adults feel good because after all we know what is right for children. We never consider that maybe we are not always right.

The look in this child's eyes concerned me so much that when I went home, I couldn't stop seeing his image over and over again in my mind. I felt we had it wrong by rendering children powerless in what could possibly be their final moments.

The following Monday after the horrible news, the staff met to discuss how we could defend our school in the event of such a tragedy.

Before the meeting, I sat there quietly even more upset from what I had seen during our drill and thoughts of what the Sandy Hook children endured flooded my mind. They were powerless against a person who had evil intent.

Teachers had been milling about prior to the meeting discussing Sandy Hook and sharing student stories of the drill. It was apparent that most of our children had heard about the tragedy and discussed their concerns earlier that day with their teachers.

One of the staff shared the anguish of a quiet 5th grade boy. He had approached his teacher and asked him when they would have permission to fight the shooter. The teacher arrogantly replied, "You don't have to worry. I will save you ... no shooter is getting past me!" The student knew that his teacher could not defend against a gun, so he replied, "What if you get killed?" Arrogantly the teacher replied, "I'm not going to let anything happen to you!" Not being satisfied with the teacher's response, the student this time decided to drop the politeness and stated what he really wanted to know: "When can we kick the bad guy in the nuts?"

When the teacher told this story, the response from others in the meeting was a roaring laugh and a statement of how cute that was and they were shocked that a sweet student such as he would even say such a thing.

Not one of the staff members understood the underlying message and concern this child was trying to communicate without being disrespectful.

It was at that moment, I realized how much power we easily take away from children in a school setting. Not only did we emotionally deprive this child of his natural instinct to fight and fend for his life but we are offering our final wielding of power over him that he must obey our directives because we said so and we have no other solutions to offer.

It was apparent the faculty was united in taking this child lightly and easily surrendered a pivotal opportunity to make a connection with students that was so important to them. I, on the other hand, had been completely changed by the Sandy Hook children and knew their voice had to speak for our 413 students.

I could no longer ignore the toxicity of the school culture and so started to pay more deliberate attention to the effects it had on our students' emotional health functioning.

The Sandy Hook children tragically witnessed firsthand the results of a young adult with mental illness who entered their school and delivered revenge with no regard for their existence.

This type of callousness should not be allowed a grooming opportunity in our school environments simply because we underestimate and downplay the feelings and emotional health issues of children.

The innocent lives of the Sandy Hook students have become the voice for American children; therefore, we must seek a way to honor their sacrifice through prevention of mental illness in early childhood so our most precious citizens are protected in their sacred space. By doing this, we become active participants in breaking the cycle of children who exhibit severe social deficits, which can become engrained violent behavior when left untreated. We cannot ever allow a student to feel their school hates them and feel their only recourse is to unleash revenge.

SECTION II

CHAPTER 16:
RESOURCE OFFICERS

Unfortunately, as more students are exposed to educational neglect during their academic career, a rise in school violence becomes a risk, as they blame the institution for compounding failures and unwanted separation from their peer group.

An officer located within the line of sight to control a hostile child or disarm an active shooter immediately is the ideal situation that would significantly decrease the number of individuals victimized.

A school campus can encompass many buildings and sprawl across a lot of acreage. An on-site resource officer ideally can be the first to respond depending on their location, the aggressor's position, and the courage of the officer.

Resource officers are a vital part of the school community and with proper training, good temperament, and a positive connection to the student body can be instrumental in making a great impact on school safety; however, assigned objectives in job duties can confuse the role in a school setting based on so many different expectations from various stakeholders, such as administrators, teachers, and the students themselves.

Some visualize the officers as being more permissive when dealing with students, and want them to model "friendship" type behavior in order to build relationships, hoping they will confide when knowledge of a serious threat is learned. Confidentiality is imperative, and factors such as the child's previous life experience with authorities and their grade level or age reflects on their willingness to come forward with information.

Meanwhile, others desire a more authoritarian presence by having the officer explicitly deal with an unruly child or most importantly to decommission an active shooter. There is a high amount of importance in expectations from each type of stakeholder, but the students have a very different perception for their needs such as requiring a more authoritative approach. The relationship is built on trust through the actions of these officers and how they handle fluid student encounters. Because most school incidents are in the public view, the "rumor mill" becomes highly influential with perception if officer behavior leads to mishandling or an overreaction in a student-involved incident. Officer training and sensitivity awareness for their own personal behaviors help build trust with students, because they have an expectation of being treated with respect and dignity during an encounter with authority.

Students should be made aware of the resource officer's role and informed they represent law enforcement. When clear guidelines are set regarding professional staff roles, this gives valuable information to students with whom to seek appropriate help when they are at a crossroads. They also can be assured through professional collaboration someone will meet their needs without falling through the cracks.

A school counselor is an integral part of building relationships with students and a necessary collaborator with the resource officer or law enforcement representative. Building this alliance and communication network allows for sharing of information on "at risk" students so proper intervention and monitoring can take place.

Because school counselors are student representatives, their collaboration with a resource officer should not be confused as enforcers of the law with students. There should be no confusion to the student on which role each professional engages.

One of the dilemmas some school districts face is whether to start their own police force or utilize the city's police department with officers designated at the school.

The quality of a resource officer is imperative for student safety. Some officers become part of a resource team because they may not be meeting expectations for law enforcement but their training makes them a good candidate for schools.

Some of these officers may have behavior issues themselves, as they could lack the ability to regulate their own impulse or easily feel the need to wield power, so placing them in an enforcement type of position with children might be "fueling the flames." Other officers may have felt bullied when they were in school themselves and could show very little tolerance when triggered by students whom they currently have identified as bullies.

Standards that seek an officer with high emotional intelligence (EI) is most favorable for student safety. A personality screener should at least be part of the qualification package to weed those who may have deficits in self-awareness, self-regulation, empathy, and social skills themselves.

If a district looks to the city for uniformed officers to place in their schools, such as in Louisville, Kentucky, how are we reassured that the quality of officers meets the high expectations and standards of being near our students?

Administrators are faced with a difficult dilemma as the Louisville Police Department has been plagued with several officers engaging in inappropriate behavior during oversight of a student explorer program. Charges of child molestation and rape were filed against some officers who were later convicted.

Unfortunately, the Louisville Police Department had other officers in a non-school setting convicted of sexual assault during the same time period. No administrative changes at the top in the had taken place to correct this most flagrant abuse and violation of the public's trust. Like all cases of predatory behavior, they are allowed to continue when those at the top protect the perpetrator(s).

We have to consider if we are so desperate that just putting a façade of officers in charge of our students' safety is "just good enough" and makes adult administrators happy they are doing something that the community has demanded to curb school violence.

Districts should consider how to protect students from culpable behavior not only if they bring city officers in the school but if they hire them directly as well.

When a school district decides to set up their own police force, they are now going into the law enforcement business and the officers will work directly as an employee. This move is not only outside the educational scope of the institution but can come with its own set of alarming considerations. By school districts hiring their own force, they have complete control over the information that is revealed to the public regarding every incident. Some controversial circumstances and events may have to rely on student videotaping in order to expose the real truth should the district act inappropriately in their investigation.

By investigating themselves and having officers as employees, a district can easily cover up an incident by securing ownership of the information and having direct access to already retained lawyers.

No matter what direction our public education system takes for implementing a program to keep our schools safe, there should be an independent citizen review board to manage oversight. This will respect student safety, ensure information is not bias to the school district or law enforcement, and demand that officers are highly selected and accountable for their behavior.

CHAPTER 17:
GUN LAWS AND VIOLENCE

Most Americans are grief-stricken when the news of a school or mass shooting is announced. It is such a senseless crime as the victims had been going about their daily lives with no indication of what was going to transpire. The shattered lives of loved ones left behind are devasted as they try to make sense of something that is so violent, irrational, and unexpected. This grief is even more unbearable when it involves the loss of children.

The decision to use a weapon against unarmed innocent victims is a selfish act that is motivated by a shooter's need to regain power and control that had been critically lost earlier.

Unfortunately, in the desperate search for answers, the community looks at politicians to enact stricter gun laws or demands more regulation. Because this is a Second Amendment Right, it has become a "hot button" issue in our country that divides the citizens by those who want more regulation and those who are gun rights advocates. We then, again, are repetitively thrown into a political debate for solving a very complex problem that is emotionally charged but legally protected.

How do we balance the seriousness of mental health issues in children that lead to gun violence in our country with the constitutional rights of our citizens to own guns, as both sides provide good arguments?

I have not seen any best evidence-based research that suggests a gun law can cure mental illness; furthermore, implying that more weapon laws will protect citizens from future shootings is not only deceptive but misleads the public in their search for appropriate action that could identify the core as a long history of mental illness that has roots started in childhood.

A mentally ill person can easily be embedded in our schools or workplace. Their harassment of others can easily create a situation where a target would want to lash out in violence putting all in the building at risk. The same can become true for a child who was bullied by school staff and felt hated by their school community.

My resiliency developed from childhood was a major reason for not using violence as a way to solve an extremely painful problem against the predator who was causing me intense life-changing harm. I had layers of protective factors such as the ability to problem-solve, regulation of impulse, planning and understanding cause and effect that kept me levelheaded. I had to use all of these strategies during my moment of crisis.

A lot of my students have already experienced a lifetime of trauma that could cause social deficits in functioning if left untreated. It's important to recognize these issues usually manifest during childhood, yet the reaction to address the emotional health problem sometimes doesn't take place until adulthood.

We have to figure out how to reverse engineer treating this neglect before engrained personality disorders take root in our young people because mental health treatment failed to arrive.

A school should not be contributors to emotional illness in children by targeting students who fail to perform or misbehave but instead promote healthy environments where they can thrive and feel part of their school community no matter their abilities.

Many students have access to guns not only in volatile household situations but in healthy homes as well. Dinner table conversations on proper handling of guns with young children, no matter what type of family dynamics, usually are stern warnings to "never touch my gun!" There is also a false belief among children that a very young sibling "does not have the strength to pull the trigger" and so it is okay in their mind for the parent to allow the child to touch the gun.

Children by nature are inquisitive, and their curiosity heightens when adults grossly dramatize the forbiddance of touching their weapon. It is not that a child wants to misbehave but because they are curious, they wish to explore further why they shouldn't.

School counselors are in a precarious position if they provide education on gun safety in a school guidance lesson. Many elementary children in a counseling session will randomly discuss an incident involving access to a weapon and how they should have handled the situation. A school counselor can provide a safe environment for a student to talk about an unsettling gun experience at home. Many discussion opportunities were initiated by my students as the town we lived was culturally a hunting area with many family traditions geared towards this type of recreation.

The problem of teaching gun safety arises with adult uncertainty because if we talk about guns to children, we feel they will be drawn to seeking them out and explore their function, thus putting them at even higher risk of injury or fatality.

Balancing adult and children gun concerns is quite difficult because they are both very valid; however, what I learned in counseling sessions with my elementary students is they are needing information and answers on dealing with finding a weapon or how to curb curiosity knowing where it is stored, especially when an adult is not around. They also express guilt in going near a weapon when their parent didn't know and express how fear of punishment keeps them from telling an adult.

I had received a McGruff gun safety program during the summer before the school year started. After previewing the disk, I believed it was most appropriate for my younger students who were the age recommended on the instructions. I knew that it would be controversial, so I didn't show it for the longest time as I weighed the benefits versus consequences.

Later in the school year, after many student concerns, I finally decided to play the program and was taken back at how focused the students were to watching the safety message. After the viewing, they asked many questions and described incidents they had been exposed to at home. The conversation also led into peer group discussion when the class was asked how they would handle the same scenario a student described.

The classroom response was not what I had expected. They were thoroughly engaged with participation in offering opinions, ideas, and problem-solving. I had been unsure in my decision to show this age-appropriate informational program but wanted my students to have valuable information they could use when no one was around to help them make a good choice.

As a school counselor, I wish there was a best evidence-based guideline to advise me in this most important controversial guidance program. No counselor should have to guess if this is a right decision or not, so I hope the American School Counseling Association (ASCA) can expand their position statement on the Prevention of School Related Gun Violence which outlines protocol for keeping the environment safe but does not include student gun safety.

Opening dialog in schools on gun safety and violence can also help identify students who may be inclined to use a weapon in a future school shooting. For example, I had a child express to me during session that he shot a dog with a gun simply because it was in his yard. He dreamed of killing a person next and fantasized during the school day of the actual killing. He could describe in detail how he thought a person's body would react when they were killed.

I referred him to an outside counseling program and notified his parent. Although his mom was concerned when she received this information, she refused to pursue treatment. I also filed a report with child services but had no other options of having him monitored.

It would have been nice to have a formal support system beyond social services where I could have sought assistance for this child, especially for the safety of our school. His emotional health and violent behavior were an extreme outlier He presented himself early as having a serious mental health issue and because of his young age, he was forthcoming with information as he enjoyed shocking others laying out the details of his fantasy.

I fear his appetite for violence will escalate as he ages because he will eventually learn to keep his plan more secret as he moves on to middle and high school. Unfortunately, as he develops more violent desires, the unaddressed mental health issues will have blended into his real world and become normal for him. We have to figure out how we can help a child like this, especially when we have caregiver denial and his symptoms may be outside the scope of available referral agencies.

CHAPTER 18:
NEIGHBORHOOD SCHOOLS

There is nothing better than having a neighborhood school for a child's sense of belonging. Having an opportunity to socialize face-to-face on their street, on the walk to and from school, or while in after-school programs allows kids to connect with a large segment of their local school community because they see them in the neighborhood.

The neighborhood school offers healthy experiences for children to build relationships without barriers of long transportation rides, limited access to technology, or organized adult-planned socializing expectations.

Children can learn through their neighborhood interactions things like rule setting, team building, tolerance, and problem-solving during unstructured play. The neighborhood school reinforces bonds for children to structure themselves and curb behaviors that may be unappealing through peer correction.

When a child is bused to another area outside the community because their neighborhood school is dilapidated, unfit, or like in Louisville, Kentucky, for diversity reasons, their sense of belonging can diminish from enduring the long ride that separates them from the neighborhood community and their local peer relationships.

The Jefferson County Public Schools (JCPS) system in Kentucky has continuously bused their children out of neighborhood schools for over thirty years and they are still doing it. They have one of the highest budgets for transportation in the nation to accommodate shuffling students to other areas of the county.

Throughout the decades, JCPS has worked hard each school year to "fine-tune" its busing plan. There are probably more administrative hours designated for this than educational planning. It takes a lot of input from the community, school board, and other stakeholders. So much time and effort are required to continue a system that should have been stopped years ago. They have already completed shipping out at least two generations of kids and have nothing to show for their efforts that positively justifies continuing this dysfunctional policy.

To support this practice of misguided intent, the property tax fees throughout the county continuously rise without citizen input, and federal tax dollars are wasted on footing an enormous transportation bill.

West Louisville is one of the top cities in the United States with the highest crime rate for murder. Most every child that grew up in that area had been bused out of the community during their educational journey.

Should we take a look at a possible correlation between crime in a certain area and the availability of good neighborhood schools that have local community investment?

We easily bus our kids out of the area by blaming the budget, stating there are simply no funds to fix the local neighborhood school or build a new modern one. I think that is a deflection from other reasons such as school districts may not have a desire or energy to come up with new strategies to invest in a local school, or they simply want to divide the students into multiple schools in order to dilute low performing test scores on state statistics.

Unfortunately, having bad schools in poor neighborhoods and parents tired of busing has left families to seek answers through their own advocacy in the media and with community churches.

Louisville parents have temporarily solved the problem by forming an all-male black school as well as separate all-female black school with school board approval. This decision was well supported by the district because it made the parents happy and gave the district two important public relations achievements. They listened to the parents' request and were not labeled "racist" because they approved the plan. This decision also once again allowed the district to defer responsibility for not investing in their neighborhood schools.

Why couldn't the school board provide our students the same enriched opportunities the parents demanded in their own neighborhood school nearby?

What do we do with the other children who were not accepted to these schools, and are we reversing back to segregation just so our black students can receive a quality education? Shame on the local district for not meeting the needs of everyone so our kids can stay local and have an expectation of receiving a quality education.

The needs of school children are very different today than decades ago. Many of our children are faced with adult problems at a very young age. Our society has become more transient with high housing cost and evictions. Two-parent families are becoming fewer and more grandparents are raising their grandchildren.

A neighborhood school helps children feel more secure because they are familiar with their surroundings and hold a sense of community. Friendships are easier to develop face-to-face as investment in each other can be achieved without barriers like long commutes or hoping one can participate in sporting programs that are only available in their far-distant school.

Our kids deserve to have a local school down the street with highly qualified teachers who want to invest in the community. There are good teachers who want to be part of a rich school culture no matter the neighborhood because the rewards of teaching are seen in the results of their effort. When educators know they are backed by positive student investment policies set by the district, they are free to focus on teaching instead of how to survive a bad work environment.

I hope citizens can get out there and fight for neighborhood schools and stop swallowing the rhetoric from "out of touch" school administrators who use "I'm really trying to help you" words when in actuality they have no evidence their dysfunctional busing policies have helped west Louisville kids succeed.

When we separate our kids from their community during their school journey, why are we surprised when they grow up with no positive attachment to the neighborhood they actually live in? Why are we further surprised when they form gangs looking for a community to belong?

CHAPTER 19:
RECESS

"It's the things we play with and the people who help us play that make a great difference in our lives." ~ **Fred Rogers**

When I was a child, I grew up in a time period when all kids were free-range. We would walk everywhere, ride our bikes, and have street football or baseball games with the neighborhood kids.

We had freedom to be amongst our peers without adults setting the rules, breaking up fights, or interfering with our somewhat organized play. If we had a conflict, we had to problem-solve right there in the moment so we could continue to play.

Times are very much different now as kids are more confined to the home, usually go with adult supervision, and have transferred their direct contact of socialization to an indirect connection through social media. Adults can easily jump in the arena to solve the child's problem and unwittingly undermine their self-esteem.

The evolvement of social media for childhood communication has become a mainstream way of learning social skills, building self-esteem, and feeling part of a peer group that can be emotionally rewarding when their post goes viral or is well liked and the responses are to the child's expectations.

The physical distancing from peers in social media can quickly go awry with misunderstandings, bullying, and the lack of ability of words to show intended expression or emotions. Perception, interpretation, and the complication of language can contribute to social media becoming risky for some children to engage, as they easily misinterpret the intended meaning. Other children feel it's a safe way to bully others because for some reason they become brave enough to inflict their message from afar than they would in person.

The social risk to children is more complicated today than ever before with the instantaneous way information can spread. Any negative aspects can create feelings of inferiority and distance a child from their peer group.

We cannot ignore that recess not only provides physical activity but offers a beneficial opportunity for kids to have direct interaction with one another to work emotionally on social awareness and develop twenty-first century skills.

Providing recess or social opportunities for students in a school setting is a great way for kids to reset during their day, release some pressure, and learn self-awareness when their peers call them out on their behavior. Recess is a great opportunity for building healthy emotional intelligence.

Free time allows for identifying conflicts, anxiety, and problems in the peer group that can be addressed in the "here and now." When kids have opportunity to express through free play or free time during school, they can become more secure amongst their peer group, as they work out issues as they arise.

As good as it sounds for kids to be allowed recess, unfortunately there are a lot of barriers that get in the way to keeping this childhood tradition alive. Some schools see recess time as an area that can be cut to only one recess a day instead of two or reduced in span, so by the time games are organized recess is over. Recess can also be viewed as a reward for good behavior or as a punishment to be taken away.

Denying access to recess for behavior students is a tool that is sometimes utilized by teachers as a threat in order to gain compliance. Some kids are lucky and have recess protected through their individualized educational plan or 504 accommodations. Kids who do not enjoy protection through these government plans are at risk of losing their recess or having a reduction in time for the day if they act up.

The weather can also be a common threat to recess and outdoor play, as it can easily be moved indoors with extreme low or high temperatures. At our school, the students were redirected to quiet indoor play for over 50 percent of the school year due to inclement weather conditions.

Having recess confined to their classroom for a majority of the school year was torturous for most kids, and behaviors would soon escalate especially towards the end of the year with all that pent-up stress.

By having recess in the classroom, it created an oxymoron for the kids because they needed relief from classroom pressure, and when they were reassigned back into the classroom for recess, there was no relief for them. It just didn't make sense. They just couldn't catch a break!

It would be a dream for every new school built today to include an indoor play area for recess that had a walking/running track, climbing obstacles, and field game area. It should also be mandated that classes not be assigned in the space that can potentially tie up access for free play.

Education is a priority, and sometimes the spirit of pushing forward is not in the best interest of students when they are not allowed to take a break from a consistent hammering of information in the classroom.

Recess needs to have protection from cuts in the school day. School culture should understand the importance of its potential to influence a positive emotional outlook for our students.

These designated periods in a child's day allow time to regroup, refresh, and work on their very needed social skills. This is also a great time for a school counselor to be available in the field to provide services for conflict resolution, anxiety coping mechanisms, and encourage compromising with their peers.

Kids who are allowed free play or have free time during their school day learn to organize games, set rules, decide fairness, and enforce compliance of the standards set by the schoolyard kids who proudly are in charge of their own play.

Kids are experts at play and love opportunity for expression. Denying a designated break during the day is like asking a young person who is developing their impulse control to sit tight through hours of material that flood their mind in the classroom. How does this contribute to a healthy emotional intelligence (EI) for our students?

Recess needs to be protected and seen as a valuable social learning tool in a positive school culture.

CHAPTER 20:
MEDICAID

My only previous experience with Medicaid was working with students at my school. It was frustrating when I had to refer a child for outside counseling services and there were very few providers accepting this government program in our area.

Adding to the problem was the availability of four different Medicaid plans and where families had to choose one during open enrollment. Unfortunately, finding a counselor who accepted Medicaid and then accepted the plan the student's family had chosen extremely narrowed down the opportunities for a child to receive services. Over 85 percent of my referrals did not have acceptable insurance that a counselor provider would accept.

Eventually an untreated student with high emotional needs would deteriorate and their explosive behavior would become a problem in the classroom. Because of the lack of referral alternatives, the only option for the student to receive treatment is inpatient hospitalization in a nearby town where they accept all Medicaid insurance plans.

This type of referral would be a temporary fix to a long-term emotional health issue the student is challenged with in their daily life. Most of our Medicaid families would not be able to complete follow-up care upon release due to transportation and financial issues associated with a commute out of the area. So now we end up repeating the same cycle of not fully helping the student; however, in the eyes of toxic school staff, having the student hospitalized allowed much-needed respite for the classroom.

Children on Medicaid are at the mercy of their parent jumping through complicated hoops, which the state requires in order to receive or maintain coverage. Just to change an address requires thirty minutes of questioning on the phone with the agency, as they want to make sure you answer all the questions correctly or you could be ineligible to continue coverage. I can understand why parents lie about where they live as the threat of benefit loss is quite real with just the changing of an address.

Incarcerated parents or those with pending legal issues can have difficulty attending to the Medicaid paperwork. Because of their failure to meet deadlines and correct previous offenses, they risk a lapse in medical coverage and so will now be mandated to complete community service before a reinstatement of benefits is allowed.

Some custodial parents would not cooperate with Medicaid because of substance abuse, and they could use the benefit as leverage against grandparents who are willing to take custody. By withholding completion of the paperwork, they can negotiate things they want like keeping any monthly disability payments the child may receive. The grandparents do not have a lot of rights while taking care of their grandchild until they have their case sent through the court system and temporary custody is issued. Meanwhile the child's medication is delayed while this legal process is working its way through the system.

I had many students who were prescribed ADHD medications by a pediatrician. These are considered a controlled substance and can only be filled 30-days apart. If the medication is "lost or stolen," the child will be forced to abruptly discontinue treatment until the next refill date arrives. The immediate termination of the drug will unfortunately have an effect on the student as they experience bizarre and unusual behavior in the classroom while they simulate a detox.

Some children will experience these vacillating mood changes on a consistent basis as their meds are continually "lost or stolen" until social services can intervene and stabilize the situation.

Unfortunately, during a simulated detox, the student lacks the ability to curb impulse or empathize with others and will not have a care in the world but will recognize their behavior is inappropriate. They will endure multiple removals from their peer group because they are so disruptive to the classroom.

Most lost or stolen prescriptions can quickly be filled if a police report is filed; however, in a lot of our cases, the parent would refuse to file because the medication had been used for other means such as sold for cash or consumed by themselves.

It is quite difficult for a Medicaid parent to obtain a sick appointment for a child on the day of illness from their primary care physician. There are many reasons for this as the office may only take a certain amount of Medicaid patients for the day or they may only take Medicaid patients on certain days of the month or simply they are just booked.

What this means is that a child on Medicaid will have to go to Urgent Care but, in our state, will have to wait until after 4:00 p.m. to be admitted or Medicaid can refuse payment for services. When the child is finally able to see a physician, they may need a prescription which more than likely can't be filled that evening because the pharmacy is closed, so the parent will have to wait until the next day.

A child who is prescribed antibiotics will need to have taken them for twenty-four hours before returning to school. This means a Medicaid child can miss up to two days more of school than his privately insured peer who was able to be examined on the same day of illness and started their antibiotics right away.

If the child's symptoms were outside the scope of the Urgent Care facility, the attending physician cannot do a referral for a Medicaid patient. The child will have to wait until they see their primary care who then can write the referral.

Recently Americans were outraged at conditions migrant children were facing in detention centers at the border like not having access to soap or toothbrushes. I would like to bring awareness to the fact that there should be equal concern for our existing low-income school children currently receiving Medicaid and SNAP benefits. They too have a commonality with the migrant children and are not able to access soap and toothbrushes under government programs.

Laundry detergents and hygiene products do not qualify as purchases either, for families. Going to a laundry facility to wash clothes is another overwhelming financial burden. School bullying incidents increase for low-income children in regard to their poor hygiene, and parents of these same children are more than likely to be patronized by school staff when they usher them out of the school due to an offensive odor.

When I became unemployed, I reluctantly was forced to become a partic-ipating member of Medicaid. I was now on the other end of private insur-ance and navigating a world in which I had no experience. My enrollment became an "awakening" to how the system actually works and how differ-ent it was from what I perceived. I had been blessed throughout the years of enjoying private healthcare coverage and now I was thrust into a world where I had to fight to even have appropriate attention to my health needs.

I believe that a person who has never been a participating member of Medicaid should never form policy or opinion on what they think is best for our low-income citizens without having true experience on how the system works first.

Most people on the Medicaid program have had an unfortunate life event that took place in their past and have experienced emotional difficulty or physical disability that rendered them unable to get beyond a specific barrier. When they become a member of a government assistance program, they are surrendering their independence and become totally reliant on them for help. This is not a good position for anyone to face, and it takes a lot of effort with many barriers to overcome in order to be released from this type of subjugation once you enter its realm.

There is also great bias and stereotyping of Medicaid patients from medical office staff and physicians. This can occur in scheduling of appointments further out than private pay. The wait to be seen by a physician for a routine physical can average five months. Most appointment schedulers will offer the nurse practitioner for services first. It is hard to have a good pool of doctors to choose from, as there is much physician dissatisfaction due to the very reduced reimbursement rate for services and the constant denial of better-quality prescriptions they prescribe for their patients. With the denials come lengthy physician authorizations detailing previously failed medications if they wish to pursue obtaining the preferred medicine for their patient. In other words, Medicaid patients have to endure several months of failure on two different medications before they are allowed approval for the preferred prescription their doctor originally wished them to have.

Medicaid will cover some over-the-counter medications with a physician's authorization, but most medical offices are unaware or ignore submitting paperwork for such an item they believe the patient should pay.

If a patient should ask medical staff for an over-the-counter item to be written on a prescription, they are more than likely to get a response from medical staff such as "it's only $7 for the medication!" This response not only embarrasses the patient but places a health burden on deciding whether they should purchase it themselves or use what little cash they have to meet other basic human needs.

All over-the-counter medicines should automatically be written as a prescription when a person is on Medicaid so the patients aren't asked to weigh the financial burden on purchasing the product. The downside to over-the-counter meds written on a prescription come with increased cost. Someone has to pay for pharmacy staff picking the product off the shelf and placing a prescription label. In my experience, I had an over-the-counter med that cost Medicaid $350 as a prescription but had I been able to retrieve it off the store shelf and purchase at the cash register with my Medicaid card, it would have only cost $35.

A Medicaid patient is more likely to hoard their prescriptions or not take the prescribed amount because of the difficulty in obtaining the medication in the first place. They also become easily discouraged with constant denial of prescription coverage. There is an underlying fear they will not have access to fill their prescriptions in the future due to the threat of benefit changes and loss. All of these factors play a role in the health deterioration of a Medicaid recipient.

I'm reluctant to tell others that I'm a participant of Medicaid coverage because of the biased conversations that have been discussed at family and friend gatherings in the past and present. The disclosure would open another wound of humiliation that I cannot endure.

Realistically I had to accept that I am now low-income, and the prospect of returning to my professional work seems so far away because of a chronic health condition that was controlled when I had private insurance and now is outside my financial means to ever be stabilized in a timely manner.

I was a person who went from a contributing member of society in the helping profession engaging in consumerism, recreation, home ownership, and meeting the needs of my family to a non-contributing member, unemployed and scrambling to at least fulfill basic human needs such as food, shelter, and medical care. I became a lost person with an anxious plight to get through the day, hour, or minute. Nothing else mattered until I had those basic human needs met, so having access to Medicaid, as limiting and humiliating as it was to me, was the carrot that kept me from falling further and landing in the street.

As most of my students had Medicaid as their primary health insurance, it was probably the same survival type feeling for their parents who were unable to obtain affordable private coverage. Even though Medicaid was limited in allowing children full healthcare in comparison to their privately insured peers, it was better than not having coverage at all.

Another government assistance for kids is the free and reduced lunch program. We hear all the time in the news about outrageous bills owed by parents on their child's school lunch account. We also hear of crazy ways schools try to encourage the parents to pay, but ultimately, the student foots the bill as the battle between parent and school erupts.

It is very clear and easy for me to understand how these bills rise quickly and eventually become impossible to pay as the accumulated charges far outreach the financial resources of our low-income families. Some of the families have a tendency to move and change schools frequently, and their debt burden follows as the schools collaborate with each other to collect the funds.

A lot of overdue charges are incurred simply because the parent has not completed a free and reduced application each school year. Life gets in the way such as incarceration, substance abuse, and custody disputes to name a few. Filling out these important applications are easily overlooked during stressful times. When a parent is finally able to attend to the application, the actual date they mark when signed is instrumental on determining the start date for benefits.

Even if the family is determined to qualify for the free and reduced lunch program, the benefit is not retroactive back to the start of the school year when the child started accruing the expenses. It begins on the date the parent finally signed the application. These accrued charges become the battleground between the parent who feels they don't owe because they qualified and the school who wants to recover funds to pay for food expenses they provided.

To add more confusion to the already free and reduced program, our state is discussing separating SNAP benefits from free and reduced. This means the child will not automatically be enrolled in the lunch program if they qualify for SNAP benefits.

The parent will be required to complete a separate application. I see this separation becoming another financial nightmare for schools and low-income families, as more paperwork and administrative hoops are required to supposedly assist families.

The Medicaid program is an enormous living breathing institution with many employees spread throughout the state. If you cannot complete your application or interview at the time of call because you are missing documentation, you will not be able to connect with the same worker again and will be required to have another person interpret what is missing. This process can happen several times as each worker determines differently your case. The workers can also have different levels of motivation or biases that regulate the amount of help they will give you. They know they possess all the power to determine whether you receive benefits or not.

Applying for Medicaid is a time-consuming complicated process with many questions and opportunities for a recipient to be disqualified.

It takes years to understand the government procedures of Medicaid on submitting paperwork and information correctly. The risk of not knowing can result in automatic denial where the process will have to be completely started over again with a new application.

Please don't judge a Medicaid recipient, as an unfortunate life event may have you standing in line next to them.

CHAPTER 21:

ARE WE GETTING OUR MONEY'S WORTH?

No doubt good teachers are underpaid while school districts consistently complain of budget constraints in order to deflect from implementing salary increases for its workers.

Then we have the public real estate owners who become exhausted with schools "jacking up" property tax, especially in cities where they are not given opportunity to vote on the increase. Forcing an automatic tax can leave a property owner with a bitter taste towards not supporting schools when each year the local districts take more of their money without approval or accountability and low wages are still in the headlines.

There are differences of opinions and perceptions on what districts thought were "good ideas" or "not so good programs" that cause the education system to continually be in a circular pattern of financial dysfunction regarding their budget and operations. Mismanaged districts like ours have high staff turnover and are continually rebuilding and restarting new programs yearly. It would be nice if districts were required to do a statistical analysis of the school staff turnover rate and report to stakeholders. I wonder if tracking turnover costs would better serve students because schools would be forced to invest in reducing staff turnover instead of accepting it as a budgeted sunk cost? Just by eliminating common termination practices in our district that noted an employee separation was "at will" would decrease the turnover rate in our district immensely.

What would happen if we paid teachers more, but we screened for a higher-quality applicant? What if we eliminated tenure and weeded out the nonproductive who enjoy protection? What if we invested in mentoring our school employees who show potential but are having a difficult time? What if the district and school board had a citizen's peer review board for oversight?

We are asking educators who are in the most powerful positions in the district to be in charge of making sound financial decisions with taxpayer dollars. Unfortunately, most school leaders do not possess a formal background in financial business applications and operations. Any financial learning usually takes place on the job.

Most highly qualified individuals whose expertise is in finance and accounting are extremely outnumbered by other educators who lack understanding of the specialized field, so more than likely the educated few eventually succumb to pressure and are forced to follow the ill-informed, uneducated financial direction of the leader in charge.

Districts can be further at risk if the funds are easily mismanaged by the financial person. Even though there may be assigned oversight, the lack of financial knowledge within the district may unknowingly allow impropriety.

This happened in our district where our financial person in charge was able to secretly embezzle one and a half million dollars over several years. It eventually was her arrogance that allowed her to be caught when a suspecting bank employee alerted the FBI to a possible impropriety. The school district had no idea the charming well-liked person in charge of district funds was covertly stealing.

There are different types of school budgets that can only be used for specific purposes, so this can create a lot of frustration in thinking there may be money, but in reality, there isn't. Money allocation in schools is a mystery that only a few privileged understand.

I would always be frustrated at the end of the year when teachers were pressured to spend their allotted money or lose it. It reminded me of a kid in the candy store where you have free rein to buy whatever you want even if it's not good for you.

This year-end rush to spend increases the chances that best purchasing choices are probably avoided because teachers are limited by spending handcuffs. They aren't allowed to rollover funds to the next school year where they could possibly purchase better-quality programs for our students.

If schools were considered a business, our students would be our product. There are many companies that invest in the quality of goods they use for resources in building their products.

A very successful business often requires high-quality goods and will go to great lengths in seeking out this resource. They know their return on investment (ROI) can yield an outstanding durable product, a great reputation along with rewards of consumer loyalty, and increased company profits. They value quality over quantity.

Some companies will invest in inferior goods to build mass products with a short diminishing rate of return in hopes the consumer will buy another one and forget their frustration about the product not lasting. The low-price lures customers in the market for these goods, as it allows them to go about life until the next failure. These consumers easily accept their buying decisions and adopt it as normal because replacement goods are always at their disposal. They value quantity over quality.

How does a toxic school system measure up? Which business model from above are they more likely to engage? Since students are the product of schools, do they value students at the center of their decision-making or have they drifted to investing in administration and teachers as their main product?

It is easy to flow money away from students when the loudest cash demands are voiced from grown-ups, so unless we can address adult needs of pay increases, pensions, classroom behavioral interventions and professional support, the students will have to wait.

Historically, one student service has remained constant over the years and that is the cafeteria. Back in the day, workers actually cooked homemade meals. Today, cafeteria dining consists of processed food that can easily be poured from a can and reheated in a microwave or pulled from the freezer and warmed in the oven.

In schools, we feed our students inferior foods because we cannot afford quality, yet we expect our return on investment to be a good healthy functioning child without sickness. We operate under a short diminishing rate of return daily with our students as we ask them to learn on empty high-calorie processed foods.

If you ever wanted to measure the impact of these supposedly nutritious foods (which meet federal guidelines) from a student perspective, go to the school office after breakfast or lunch and count how many kids are throwing up. This also has an effect on their academics, as they are forced to leave school for the day until their temporary illness from ingesting inferior food subsides.

Proper nutrition can be a catalyst in the learning process that helps feed the brain in absorbing information and provide the body energy to function in a healthy manner, yet no importance is given to student health when cafeterias continually feed them low-grade foods. Once again, we are disrespecting our students because of our inability to understand the connection to learning and demand quality nutrition for their well-being.

Cafeteria food will always be a negative childhood rite of passage that will remain in the crosshairs of funding. A student's nutritional needs during the school day can become a soft target for school districts to easily overlook and limit their investment on delivering better-quality food.

Schools play a heavy role in the potential future outcome of our young citizens simply because education can be a protective factor for prevention in making bad choices. I challenge every city to look at the crime rate, incarceration percentages, drug related activities, poverty, and gun violence and then notice which school district operates in those high-risk areas, and you will probably see a correlation with a toxic school district that is not accountable to students nor cares of the quality child they pass along to the community.

When I evaluated our small town with these rates, I felt ashamed because I know schools play an active role in these outcomes because we are the ones educating the citizens of our area. Almost every child that lived in our town went to one of our district schools.

The schools must accept some accountability for the social failure in these statistics because no one else has as much access to influencing children growing up other than caregivers.

What if we skimmed some money off the top? I always thought it was odd that in the schools we struggled to make ends meet but in administration they were growing like crazy and hiring more staff to help the schools with the problems created by underfunding. Isn't this an oxymoron?

When it comes to underfunding, another hot button topic is the pension system. This is a complicated program that is based on employees contributing and school districts funding. It is a pyramid system that requires more employees to contribute than those who are drawing retirement.

It is a system that has a retiree's account depleted to zero from withdrawals on the average of five years after retirement. It is a system that most teachers don't understand yet will gladly fight, protest, and willingly be tossed into the throes of passion to defend by their union.

Abuse of the pension system can easily occur by toxic districts who fail to allow state pension system employees to access their records for audit and validate they are accurately contributing. A toxic district will hire lawyers to block access to pension employees when they are not abiding by the laws set forth by the retirement plan; furthermore, these same types of districts will underfund their share by requiring some employees to remain temporary long term so they are not obligated to contribute the employer's portion.

I was a temporary employee myself for almost two years before my district would allow me to have full-time status and be eligible for benefits. My sister-in-law was a temporary employee over twelve years in her school district.

School employees should understand the workings of the pension system instead of relying on the teacher's union and the school district to drive their knowledge through fears.

If one understands basic math, they can reconcile the problem with underfunding of the pension system through their own paychecks by calculating what they contributed during their employ and combine with district contributions. They will notice there was only a lifetime of combined contributions that were less than 30 percent of their wages. When the employee expects to fully receive near their final salary upon retirement, there is close to a 70 percent deficit in funding, thus resulting in a system that cannot sustain itself unless new membership drastically far outweighs current retirees.

To add further insult to the pension system is when school districts contract services instead of hiring directly. The contracted person is usually a retired school employee collecting their pension with the added benefit of drawing a contract salary near what they were making when employed. Since they are "contracted," they do not contribute to the pension plan.

These "double-dippers" are a way for districts to covertly show an act of defiance in funding the pension system. Because contracted employees are exempt from providing a pension contribution, this means the district does not have to fund their portion. This is another way for districts to save money, but how does it contribute to offering a secured retirement benefit to our teachers?

I too was a drain on the pension system when I was terminated abruptly. I had ten more years to add to the pension with my salary, but out of necessity had to take early retirement after my dismissal. I also had worked many of my vested years in a classified status with a low salary but finished out in a certified status with a high salary, thus spiking my monthly income to be received.

We really need to figure out if we are getting our money's worth by prioritizing our needs and eliminating waste. Running the schools like a top-notch company would definitely yield a better product that everyone could be proud of and our community would benefit immensely.

Our students deserve respect by viewing them as a very worthy investment, and they should be at the center of the business model in decision-making. This is how we build a great student one individual at a time!

CHAPTER 22:
VINCENT VAN GOGH

"Art is to console those who are broken by life." ~ **Vincent Van Gogh**

It is imperative we understand the workings of hate because it is the most emotionally devastating act one can inflict on another human being. No one is exempt from becoming a target, especially if they have talent.

Hateful acts towards another have been around for centuries and have affected some of our most famous pioneers in history.

I was always intrigued by the story of Vincent van Gogh because he eventually became labeled a "madman," and this overshadowed his talent throughout life. I often wondered if he was driven to psychological isolation from sociopathic behavior inflicted by another person(s)?

There were many rumors and speculation about Van Gogh's mindset, especially after he cut off his ear. What would drive such a person to do such a drastic act?

Historians have examined his life and claim some of the evidence shows that Van Gogh was a target of two individuals that were connected to his landlord. The landlord wanted him out of the housing unit so developed a scheme to pursue his goal from "behind the scenes" without harming his own reputation. He hired two alleged deviates who began to rally others in accepting a projected image of Van Gogh as a "crazy person."

The consistent repetition of spreading a rumor about the talented artist soon captured a small force of believers who quickly grew to including most of the townspeople. This hatred directed towards Van Gogh would eventually drive him out of his home giving the landlord exactly what he wanted.

Historically, Van Gogh had been a social person until the landlord's deception. In his effort for self-preservation, he fled the area and buried himself in his work. His dream was to gain acceptance as a skilled artist and prove his value to the professional art world.

Although, Van Gogh's resilience drove him to recover and continue his work in a new town, his fractured self-esteem followed him without respite. He was unaware that his artistic talent was a threat to others that were not as talented as he. He had a humbleness that would become exploited as a weakness making him a vulnerable target. This unfortunately would keep him at risk once again when he unsuspectedly developed a friendship with another famous artist who used charm and manipulation to gain his trust.

In this relationship, Van Gogh revealed a new painting technique that had never been seen before and expressed how much it would change the art profession with this new elevated way of painting. The problems of the past were behind him as he was now on his way to becoming a respected master so he thought.

Unfortunately for Van Gogh, he easily trusted the famous painter as they shared commonality in their art and he treated Vincent with warmth and care unlike in his previous town where they were hateful. This made it difficult for him to notice that his new friend possessed an inflated ego from being a top master artist himself.

After working together, the artist quickly realized the magnitude and brilliance of Van Gogh's artwork and the impact it would have on his own reputation. Vincent's extreme talent would threaten his artistic skills and deem them inferior as well as overshadow attention he adorned by his reputation as a master artist. This could not be allowed to happen and so once again, Van Gogh became a target to be discredited through a public smearing. He was back again to being labeled a "crazy man!"

I believe this relationship devastated Van Gogh who innocently believed in the friendship not only due to their commonality as artists but as collaborators in expanding advanced techniques throughout the art world. I think Van Gogh had viewed himself as someone who was globally promoting art to share with the world and not individually promoting himself. His counterpart, on the other hand, was an individual that relished in feeding his own ego and wanted total credit for the new technique.

I feel Van Gogh's psychological downfall was fostered by the impact of being a target not only once but twice. These emotional unprocessed traumas had to contribute to his distorted view of self by eventually believing the "attacker's" perception that he was crazy.

The "haters" had been successful in convincing a lot of people to accept the distorted "crazy" public reputation they had projected about him, so how could he ever overcome such a perception? He became a human being that could no longer feel alive so merely was existing in a lonely world.

Effective "predatory behavior" has massive power and can transform a healthy talented individual into an emotionally fragile person. The destructive consequences of annihilating one's reputation buries talent in a sea of darkness and drowns their voice.

The many seeds of hatred planted by a predator sprout internal destruction within the target as they look inward for their own accountability. This hatred infects their personality and forces a target to retreat inward with no hope of rescue.

Vincent had protective factors such as perseverance and problem-solving, but they were rendered useless when attacked by hatred. Unfortunately, his empathetic response would harbor the negative emotions that were delivered to defame his good name and tear apart his worldview.

His trusting of others was now considered a weakness when he realized that not everybody had good intentions like him. The precious possessions of unconditional trust and talent had been stolen from him and replaced with never trusting anyone again or believing he deserved to be a master artist.

I feel Vincent van Gogh only experienced or felt his true value as a talented brilliant artist for only a moment in time and was left with feelings he wanted to give more but knew it was no longer possible.

Towards the end of Vincent van Gogh's life, his worldview had drastically changed about humanity, and it was devastating to him that evil people existed in everyday life appearing like ordinary citizens without a care in the world whether you lived or died.

They could skillfully con others into accepting a false impression. If many people could believe he was a crazy maybe they were right because nothing made sense anymore. Being a target had changed the rules of normalcy, and where could he go from there?

He was driven to believe he was not worthy to pursue happiness and earn a living as an artist. It had to be unbearable for him to realize the final caveat of his life was how a few individuals had wielded power over him to personally destroy his reputation and deprive him of earning a living in their pursuit of hatred.

This unconscionable, immoral, and unethical behavior from those who are out for their own gain was too hard for Vincent van Gogh to understand,

and he lacked the skills like most targets to make sense of how such a thing could happen and furthermore, why?

He never was able to realize you can't use logical thinking on an illogical act, so the answers to the attack would never be found. He thought he could outrun the pathology by moving away but hadn't realized it had followed him and became his only world.

By now, his fragile self-had allowed evildoers to capture their "win" as he transferred the joy of living to accepting only existence for his final time on earth.

Vincent van Gogh had stacked-up trauma from being a target of hate by the time he cut off his ear. Did he do such a horrific mutilation to feel if he really was alive? Was he symbolically surrendering to his attackers in a horrific way to stop their assault, or was Vincent van Gogh truly crazy like his reputation stated?

CHAPTER 23:
COUNSELOR ROLE AND CODE OF ETHICS

Being a target from an incompetent predatory principal was extremely hard to handle, but having an additional accomplice behind the scenes projecting to be an "innocent bystander" was his "friend." She was supposed to be one of us. She was certified in my profession, so there was an expectation of ethical informed behavior on my part. Counselors are not trained to enable dysfunction.

She clearly was an accomplice and was part of the "package" when his "wrecking ball" destroyed two schools to get her on board. The thought of handing my students over to an unethical person claiming to be a counselor was an overwhelming force, which I knew I had no control over. It felt like I was fighting a custody battle for 413 kids, and there was no due process, ethics, or morals to be considered. Our students had no rights for protection while the adults were fighting.

The friend who had been lying in wait two years kept an arm's length distance at her school as a teacher covertly working with the predator and his team until the task at hand was accomplished giving her the position she needed.

It appalled me that we would have a person like that in our profession. How could her behavior not have an impact on children who were in her care if she were the school counselor? She has flawed thinking in believing it is okay to participate in covert bullying tactics, especially since she will be delivering guidance lessons to students asking them not to employ such behavior. WHAT HYPOCRISY! In my mind, she was no better than the predator as they shared common traits.

What would precipitate a certified school counselor to engage in unethical behavior, and should we trust such a person to teach values and good citizenship to students? Would she even have the temperament to protect children from harm? How did she not get "weeded out" in her counseling program?

How did she give herself permission to linger behind the scenes supporting predatory behavior in order to achieve her goal? Only she knows her moral compass. I, on the other hand, believe this was the act of someone desperate. I felt her youth and lack of life skills easily sucked her into a toxic relationship that nurtured her desperation.

Available school counseling positions are somewhat scarce especially in our district. This type of unethical practice in stealing another's position can become acceptable in small, enmeshed counties throughout the state of Kentucky when a sitting counselor has not reached tenure.

Targeted counselors become "high-risk" for this type of invasion when tenured employees wield power and have political influence to overtake their position. This also happens with non-tenured teachers who may have a more "desirable school" or "scarce" position that a tenured teacher wishes to secure. This practice is an ugly scar on the education system as a whole and can destroy a good workforce when it doesn't protect employees from becoming a target.

I am in no way excusing the "friend's" behavior and willingness to jeopardize student safety as well as their academic and emotional health, but I would like to drive the point home that she probably needed a counseling position quickly to acquire the necessary hours to maintain certification before the five-year expiration of the certificate.

Our profession has to look at why this occurred and acknowledge that more than likely this is not an isolated incident but a hidden practice from those who are starting to feel the crunch of limited positions available and needing experience to maintain certification.

It is my hope for the future there are career ladders for school counselors that would provide access to more job opportunities and drive in the direction of providing mental health services for our students.

As a school counselor gains experience, avenues for obtaining licensure as a mental health therapist would not only immensely benefit students but also provide revenue for a school when they are allowed to bill for services like speech, occupational, and physical therapy. Even the school nurse is able to bill for services, so why not mental health counselors?

There are nontraditional needs in our communities that a certified school counselor can be extremely beneficial in connecting a student's real-life world to the school. I can see school counselors expand their practice to working with alcohol drug treatment facilities where so many parents are victims of substance abuse and have children who are affected. I can see how the juvenile justice system could use school counselors to help incarcerated students overcome barriers that drove them away from their school setting. I can see prisons utilize the services of a school counselor for helping incarcerated parents become more involved and not fearful of the education system, which their child attends. I can see the local police force utilize school counselors in the field where high crime occurs with juvenile offenders in their neighborhoods. There are so many areas where someone who is specialized in the education field and possesses counseling skills can be a part of serving our communities in a nontraditional way.

In the meantime, I wondered if this "friend" had violated the American Counseling Association's (ACA) or National Board of Certified Counselors (NBCC) Code of Ethics by her unethical behavior and found there was no mention of counselor-on-counselor bullying, so I do want to suggest the following to these organizations:

ACA: add to **Section D Relationships w/Other Professionals** an additional subsection **D.1.j.** stating: *"Counselors, do not engage or participate directly or indirectly in bullying of another counselor to obtain a position."* **NBCC:** should add to their code of ethics the same statement under **"NBCC's recognize their behavior reflects on the integrity of the profession as a whole, and thus, they avoid actions which can reasonably be expected to damage trust."**

The school counseling position has usually evolved throughout history to provide services needed for the time period. With the increase in violence, racism, homelessness, poverty, domestic violence, incarceration, substance abuse, and deaths of young parents from overdoses, the evolving counseling role has had difficulty keeping up the pace in meeting the needs of students. Administrators in charge of districts lack awareness in connecting these very serious mental health issues to the effects on learning. It is not because their school counselors lack training but because of the barriers in the education culture itself.

The education system still views counselors as service providers for class scheduling, college counseling, cheerleaders at pep rallies, handing out pizza at parent events, and parking lot patrol to name a few.

These traditional and normally accepted job duties take away from student emotional needs, become a waste of counselor time, and can be fulfilled by other clerical individuals. There is a need to reframe the role of school counselors.

Providing emotional health counseling in the school setting should be a staple of every school in America. Supporting the school counselor to perform counseling duties in which they are trained as a first priority can have a profound impact on children throughout their life.

The culture of my school district discouraged counseling students and viewed the practice as "walking a fine line" because of legal liability reasons; furthermore, teachers did not want to give up instruction time and believed they could handle the child's issue in the classroom. There was also an underlying message that if a teacher sent a student to the office, they would become known for having bad classroom management skills. Unfortunately, this accepted practice in our schools disrespects the mental health needs of a child in a timely meaningful way and diminishes the clinical significance of their issue.

Providing emotional health services to children in a school setting is the best place and time for affective change. If we look at it like a medic on the battlefield, we know that many lives were saved because they were present at the moment of need.

Children live in the here and now. The best time to deliver emotional coaching is when they are distressed and allowed a safe environment to express their needs to a certified school counselor who can help them through their real-life situation.

Reaching students at a critical age in development, such as in elementary level, could have a significant impact when they become middle and high school students; furthermore, the long-term effects could positively impact their adult functioning in the future.

Another barrier to a certified school counselor's role lies within the accepted job framework outlined by educational departments throughout our states. Traditionally, school counselors were mostly teachers that evolved to the more advanced role when they received their master's degree in school counseling.

If you look at most job position frameworks from state education departments describing the school counselor role, their job function appears as a small addendum to the teacher's framework of preferred outlined duties.

The school counseling profession should disconnect from the teacher framework and have its own identity in our schools. Until this barrier is addressed, the role of the school counselor will always be viewed as a teacher's role with "other assigned duties." This is a reason why the task of counseling students becomes listed as one of the last job duties on their job description after all other clerical, teaching, or administrative duties have been addressed. Counseling students as a major portion of the school counselor's job is an "effective use" of counselor time.

I would like to see professional counseling groups such as the Kentucky Counseling Association (KCA), the American Counseling Association (ACA), and the National Board of Certified Counselors (NBCC) form together a task force to educate school districts on the role and use of school counselors in the United States.

It would be beneficial to advertise to children through public service announcements (PSA) in the media advocating for students to seek out the services of school counselors to assist them with their emotional health needs.

I would also like to see an education campaign for stakeholders to understand the type of service other helping professions in schools provide—for instance, social workers, school psychologist, and family resource personnel. Our superintendent had difficulty understanding the different credentialing and skill set each of these professions provided, and this lack of awareness appears systemic throughout the school community.

When school-based professionals are requested to unknowingly cross over into each other's lane, this breaks the collaboration relationship that is vital to providing the most beneficial services to our students. In a positive school culture, administrators respect the scope of practice for each credential and know they are building effective team collaboration for their students.

A student-centered school district creates a positive culture where children are entitled to have a full-time counselor to assist them with their emotional health needs. These types of districts don't allow "other assigned duties" to become barriers to student success.

CHAPTER 24:
TRAUMA STACKS UP

For some people emotional trauma can develop into a latent stack of "unfinished business" which started with negative childhood exposures. That was me. Unfortunately, this baggage would rear its ugly head later in life when I least expected.

Just surviving stressful events throughout my life span was good enough for me, so I parked the "injury" deep in the back of my mind; unfortunately, this did create a false narrative that "all is well."

This dysfunctional coping style not only gave me an erroneous belief of survival but had a backhanded way of deflecting how it affected my decision-making abilities and various relationships later on in life. Basically, as a result, I had very low self-esteem that was easily covered up by the "fighter" in me, and I accepted maltreatment as a normal part of life.

As the years progressed, I ignorantly continued on my way still carrying deep emotional baggage and cheating myself of proper understanding of why dysfunctional people felt normal in my life. It was familiar and everyone had drama around them, so why should I be different? I accepted these narcissists into my world and innocently allowed them to have their way because that is how it's always been.

My brain experienced an emotional rewiring from starting life out being bullied. Later on, I became an adult still using those old juvenile coping strategies. I was easily convinced that what occurred didn't happen, because as a child, I couldn't persuade anyone to understand what was happening behind the scenes, so I stopped questioning the assault and accepted this was the way of life.

As this new trauma from the predator stacks on the deck, it brings a myriad of symptoms that are overwhelmingly flooding my thoughts.

I desperately needed a paradigm shift that would destroy my childhood strategy of easily accepting a problem and ignoring the impact. It is imperative that I replace this dysfunctional blueprint I had carried forever and replace it with effective evidence-based tools learned from my profession.

Most of my protective factors had become deeply wounded from dealing with the predator because they did not have a stable foundation to support wholly my emotional health. Jagged cracks had broken through to allow anxiety, loss of trust, fight or flight, depression, suicidal thoughts, low self-worth, embarrassment, guilt, sabotaging self, fear, sleep disruption, and narrowing of people whom I would ever allow to come close to me again.

The weight of carrying this unfinished business into adulthood wasn't understood until the "final straw or breaking point" was delivered by the predator. As a result, it gave me continuous flashbacks of people who had chipped at my self-esteem throughout life, such as growing up with a brother who had a conduct disorder and marrying a spouse who was emotionally toxic.

When I added it up, I had spent almost forty years living in noxious environments and had blindly thrown away my young life that should have been a time for exploration, discovery, and the pursuit of happiness. Instead, my faulty coping mechanism had conditioned me to accept low self-worth, oppression, and micromanagement from those who I thought had more power than I could have ever possessed.

As the traumas became parked further behind over the years and started to dull, I became educated through life skills and more confident in my abilities to take care of myself, but that ride was not going to last as my luck would eventually run its course when the most severe dysfunction would strike me unexpectedly through the predator.

My education, life experience, and protective factors were not saving me any longer. I wanted to go back in time and figure out the spell cast over me during childhood that allowed narcissistic people to be drawn to me like a magnet.

As a kid, I was at the mercy of adult protection and that didn't happen. As a young adult, I was typical of someone who thinks they can fix a badly broken marriage only if I tried harder. With the predator, I was dumbfounded. My toolbox of handling the assault was empty. There wasn't even a clue on how to deal with a narcissist who hated my existence.

In my previous experience with my brother and spouse, I learned disarming them through giving attention and agreeing they were right. But "hell no," I was not going to settle for that anymore in dealing with this predator. Besides that, hatred does not want attention, it wants a win.

Recovery could be possible when there are answers to my past. In order to go forward, it was necessary to look back. Thus, my journey began on dissecting my life which included intimately understanding the bad actors that I allowed to have so much joy from my misery. It was important to rewrite my future narrative so I can fully enjoy healthy emotional intelligence. Exploring the root cause of this predator and interpreting his reason for having a hate bucket should help me understand the makings of this evildoer. By unlocking the complicated answers to him should open the door to understanding the earlier narcissists that played a leading role in my life. Each one had different motivators, but the goal of their actions was the same. They needed to have control and feel power, and I needed to figure out why it was so easy for them to make me their prey.

I had never faced the reasons why I am who I am until this last emotional assault. The predator had a profound effect on my existence because that is what he was attacking through his hatred. Even though I can never undo his actions, I do have the power to reclaim my life fully. My endgame was to find out who I was and come to believe the predator would no longer matter.

Searching for a root cause meant understanding him first and then deeply exploring my own emotional history and how I developed a particular pattern of behavior. It was important to interpret the relationship with my brother and how it played a role in the selection of a spouse who was just as abusive.

One of the key components of my dysfunction was accepting a habitual liar's answer to my questioning of their behavior directed towards me. In other words, when they told me what I saw was not true and they denied their role, the minimizing forced me to accept they were right, because I had no recourse. It wasn't until later in life I would find there was a definition for this type of behavior and that abusive people use this method to control a relationship.

It's called "gaslighting" where a person convinces you are wrong in your perception and eventually believing they are right. In other words, you are crazy and they are not. You eventually become convinced of internal craziness and question your own thinking as the repetitive emotional abuse puts layers of faulty perceptions on top of your worldview until you submit to surrendering your existence.

Unfortunately, I learned this information way too late, so it took a long time to understand the manipulation was about power and control. Adult liars are common in schools, so I would carefully weigh the pros and cons of calling them out. Sometimes it might be favorable to confront them because the risk would be low, but most of the time, it was just easier to ignore their personality deficit unless it was detrimental to a student.

There are many ways an educator can slide in their agenda as in the following event: One day I happened to see a note on the school secretary's desk, and it stated one of our students could go home with an older male teacher. The note was written by the teacher not the parent. I thought that was inappropriate because the student was a special needs third grader and no student should ever go home with a teacher by themselves, especially without their parent supervising or knowing. It also opens the teacher to liability.

I informed someone of authority over me about my concern, and they completely defended the teacher saying it was appropriate. Since the supervisor had responded like I was acting ridiculous over the student's well-being, I was embarrassed and felt my concern was invalid and definitely would be more cautious in the future. This feeling came from years of being gaslighted in relationships.

This student continued riding home with the teacher and visiting for extended periods at his house for weeks, then suddenly was stopped at the parent's request. It was hard for me to get past the purpose of this little boy with special needs spending so much time alone with this teacher. I was never privy to why the parent finally stopped the after-school connection with the teacher but I could only guess. A couple years later, this same teacher became a lead player on the predator's team. He made it clear he wanted me removed from my position.

It wouldn't be long until another inappropriate incident occurred. I happened to be cutting through the neighborhood by the school board on a weekend and noticed our technology guy was walking with a big five-gallon gas can. I stopped and asked if he needed a ride, and his response was, "You didn't see me." I looked at him oddly and brushed it off that he is just acting weirder than usual. Less than a half hour later, I was working out at a fitness center and he comes in the building reeking of gasoline. I asked him to go outside because the smell was overwhelming and further stated, "Did you spill gas all over yourself?" His response once again was, "Shush, you didn't see me!"

After my workout, I left the fitness center and noticed at the school board across the street there were police cars all around. I called my cousin who also worked in technology to inquire what was happening at the board. Apparently, someone had doused the entire inside of the building with gasoline, and the bulk of the fuel was poured on the finance person's desk.

I knew the two technology guys had been fighting over the finance person on who was going to date her even knowing she was married. They were both immature idiots fighting over a married woman. I told my cousin his "techie" coworker was the one who poured the gasoline everywhere and explained my incident with him minutes before the event. My cousin's response was that of a typical liar, and he forcibly stated that his coworker would never do something like that and he further reprimanded me for even thinking that way.

Since no one had been hurt in the dousing and insurance covered the $80,000 of damages, I did not come forward with my information because I had to deal with my cousin every day at work. His battle with the other tech guy to win over the finance person would remain a secret with me, so I protected him as that is what I am conditioned to do.

A couple years later, natural consequences would become a factor as that same finance person was the one who embezzled one and a half million dollars from the school district. The arsonist technology guy who insisted I never saw him was the one who gave the predator my email password so he could alter or change responses. As for my cousin, he refused to speak to me ever again.

Habitual liars are unscrupulous people who don't like being challenged, so in my cousin's reaction he ramped up punishment for my questioning of his affair and his coworker's gas spreading by ignoring me for years even though we worked in the same building. It seems dysfunction does run in the family line.

Looking back at my childhood from a school counselor's perspective, I ask myself how would I have identified a child like me who had early childhood trauma but didn't exhibit any behavior issues at school? How could a school counselor have made a difference in changing my narrative early in life that was more emotionally healthy? - *Later in life as a school counselor myself, I see how some children fall through the cracks as I was responsible for 413 students which is over the 250 students per counselor recommended by the American School Counseling Association (ASCA). There just wasn't enough time to service everyone.*

I was a kid who was dedicated to holding the family secrets because the threat of letting them out was far scarier than the actual assault.

Emotional trauma is not visible when you become an expert at covering up the effects and inadvertently protect those whom you cannot escape. Children wear masks to shield themselves from harm because they have no other tools to utilize. There is a critical need to protect them from covert predators in their school because they have absolutely no chance in defending themselves when they become a target.

Increasing awareness about emotional predatory behavior, especially in our schools, can help children as a preventive measure because if the illness is recognized by many, predators will finally become limited in their opportunities to become so destructive.

They are a mental health saboteur. I wonder if they had been given opportunity themselves during childhood to receive appropriate treatment, if the intervention would have allowed a better chance of correcting faulty thinking before it became so engrained.

Child targets of emotional predators deserve to have the damaging effects that were inflicted on them recognized and receive appropriate treatment tailored to this type of assault. *The Diagnostic and Statistical Manual (DSM-V)* is very hopeful for future treatment, as they look into expanding the diagnosis of post-traumatic stress disorder (PTSD) and include the subgroup complex PTSD. This is a fairly new field in psychology, so I hope consideration in the diagnostic criteria is given to "a target of bullying at school, home, or workplace" so victims of an emotional hate attack can receive proper treatment that is understood and recognized by the professionals.

CHAPTER 25:
HOW DO I FIND HELP?

Having a strong emotion towards being a single parent wasn't something I much thought of until I crossed paths with the predator. Before that resiliency, independence, and goal setting was a staple of my life. It didn't matter that I was single. "I got this" was my internal dialog; that most issues could be handled just fine. I felt confident in many aspects of life, especially in the last few years when everything seemed to be falling in place before the predator's arrival.

When this nonhuman entered my space, everything changed. I had really never deeply questioned my existence in this world until I met him. The annihilation of my soul left me clinging to search for any scraps that met my basic human needs. I had never calculated how much it costs for me to be alive each day, but now it was in my face because all my liquid cash was gone. My value was reduced to thinking if life was even worth living, especially since it was so costly.

Of course, this was a distorted way of measuring myself, but I had just come off an entire school year where I was given daily reminders that my existence as a human being had no worth.

I had been attacked, not in the open but behind the scenes. Describing what was happening seemed too involved. It dealt with many twists, turns, and multiple situations that individually seemed coincidental but collectively very dark and sinister. Who could I privately disclose what was happening to me and our students without sounding paranoid, repetitive, or ridicules?

There would be conversations with loved ones which in my case were my adult children, close family members, and friends. I would tell my story on what is happening in generalized statements that appeared "so what." I would repeat, repeat, and repeat the same nonsense to anyone who would listen, and when that didn't work, I would complain to strangers.

My situation fell on deaf ears, and in my mind if they couldn't understand the generalized part of my story, how could I even be given the opportunity to express painful details of what was truly happening?

I couldn't stop pleading my case even though I desperately wanted to quit the story vomit that was coming out of my mouth. This uncontrolled repetition left those in my path annoyed and wish I'd move on. Unfortunately, their inattentive response made my repetition worse. The more loved ones discounted my situation, redirected my conversation, the more I felt withdrawn and devalued. This minimizing of feelings made it easier to believe the predator was right in targeting me.

There was no equilibrium, as I was stumbling in every direction. My sad existence was everywhere. All relationships such as my profession, family, and friends were all on life support, yet I still could not stop the urge to tell my story.

This circular pattern of thought went on for days, weeks, months to even years. I hated that I became a stuck needle on a record player and didn't know how to stop. I was annoyed and disgusted at myself and felt the only way to break the vicious cycle was to withdraw from people so I could possibly stop the madness of reoffending myself and annoying others.

I was unfairly seeking validation from family and friends. They had no idea of the depth of my trauma, but because they heard a few "sound bites," it was enough for them to know that I was emotionally affected by what happened. They had accepted my pain from that moment but that wasn't what I was seeking. I wanted validation and complete understanding of the entire picture of what happened to me and my students. I wanted to tell our story completely.

I'm sure it never occurred to them how I would interpret their disengagement as not caring but when you are broken, words are hard to put together.

Fantasizing seemed to make a better world, so I wished there was a caring spouse by my side to fully express my grief, feel my hurt, or understand the burden of extreme economic loss; however, the reality of the situation constantly reminded me I was alone and searching for emotional rescue which wasn't going to happen. I desperately needed help from a caring person.

When I was a child, asking my mom for help was a disappointing memory. I seemed to complain to her often because I didn't know how to handle my violent older brother that was twice my size.

Crying a lot became a daily occurrence when he would physically overpower me and deliver a suffering assault. The constant tears and complaining annoyed my young mother, so she eventually became immune to my pleas for help. Finally, the last straw broke and she told me to quit whining to her for my problems. She further expressed that I would just need to "figure it out on my own!"

I remember feeling extremely sad at her response and felt abandoned. Who would help me if my mom wouldn't? It felt like the umbilical cord had been severed because I was so attached to her. After several days of moping, I had to accept her advice whether I liked it or not. She had drawn a clear boundary that I needed to figure out how to survive "the creep" in the house.

Having my mom throw me to the wolves actually did make me stronger. I learned strategies to keep a distance from my brother, like taking a different route through the neighborhood when I saw him in the area so he wouldn't commandeer my bike. I had already endured interceptions too many times, as he always forced me to ride on the back of the seat while he drove. He would speed up when we arrived at our house and stir the bike towards the maple tree then jump off at the last second leaving me to take an injurious impact.

I learned skills that he valued like fixing and repairing his bicycle because it was always broke. I especially enjoyed it when he had a flat tire because I was the only one with those repair skills. My makeshift workshop in the garage allowed me to be free from harm at the moment; however, on non-repair days, I learned how to run extremely fast and what distance I needed for safety before he would give up chasing me. My early running experience earned me many track-and-field ribbons during the school years. I also learned to read his face and hear his threats before each danger strike to limit my liabilities.

As I aged, the skill of asking for help became easily diluted and eventually faded. There was so much daily drama and trauma during childhood which forced me to navigate the best I knew how. The old saying "use it or lose it" held true for me because even the thought of asking for help seized to enter my mind as I grew older.

Unfortunately, I also diluted my listening skills when it came to others giving me advice about anything. It was in my nature to help people and it felt rewarding, but when it came to others helping me, I felt extremely uncomfortable. Their assistance was genuinely given but my reception of their gift was awkward and foreign and so I would find excuses to deflect so they would quit paying attention to me. Figuring things out on my own made me "falsely" confident. There was an underlying "trust issue" I had developed that served as the base of my problem-solving skills. Why would anyone advise me and have concern for my well-being? "What did they want in return" became my internal dialog.

Unfortunately, my childhood inability to ask for help interfered with my adult desire to seek professional counseling services in the aftermath of the predator.

I very much wanted to talk to a mental health counselor but had been left with a state of mind in not being able to define my situation. It's not that I had no idea what happened to me; it was that the whole experience was unexplainable. It didn't make sense, so I didn't even know where to start my story. I had already tried to describe my experience to many people with no avail. There was absolutely no way I was going down that rabbit hole again, especially by now I was beyond exhaustion and just couldn't stop crying.

Even though my internal desire was to get professional help, it was my routine of figuring out answers on my own that I would fall back on. I knew this wasn't the best way but it was the familiar way.

CHAPTER 26:
PLEASE DON'T LET ME LAND IN THE STREET

Losing my job, for some reason, felt like it happened so fast even though I was expecting it since the beginning of the long school year. It seemed the actual firing had dragged on so much I had forgotten the "official" termination hadn't happened yet.

The predator relished in the fact he had some dessert to deliver and that was my "pink slip." Being such a dramatic person, he probably thought I had no idea he would fire me because after all, I am really stupid! That's why terminating me at the last minute would be even more tantalizing because I might be "surprised" giving him even more satisfaction. This was necessary in case I needed a friendly reminder of his complete power over me.

I'm sure he had rehearsed this final curtain call all year long. His cloak-and-dagger moment was well worth the wait as it built suspense that allowed him to take his final curtsy in the play he had orchestrated. He was to hold the trophy of my existence in his hand with glory to show he had won.

I was in my office packing up materials for a guidance lesson, which was about to start in a few minutes when the predator had made one of his unexpected visits to my office. He proudly had my performance review in his hands with hours to spare before the termination deadline.

He had marked every box as "excellent," which I knew probably even made him want to throw up. Knowing he had plans to fire me, especially since he purposely collected stacks of discipline write-ups throughout the year, I thought it very odd that he would give me an "excellent" performance review, so I wanted to look it over and figure out what "the catch" might be. This twist was crazy, but I expected it from him as it was in line with all the other weirdness he had done throughout the year.

Politely, I informed him that I would review the papers when I returned from teaching class. My response was not what he had planned. He expected me to sign it right away, because I didn't, I could see his internal volcano starting to erupt as he abruptly left my office and then directly made a "U-turn" at the threshold returning right back in front of my face. I guess he felt that I was the one controlling him in his glorious moment of dishing out dessert, and he didn't like it one bit, so he returned with fury to retrieve his power.

He stated to me, "I don't know what your issue is and why you don't trust me, so I'm not going to renew your contract!" I thought to myself "no shit!" as I looked at him with absolutely no response. He stared me down intensely as if to try to intimidate and hopefully ignite an emotional reaction.

He had the maturity of a fourth grader with his staring tactics of trying to see who would blink first. The only thing that was missing is he could have stomped his feet and said, "I'm your principal and I said so!" Now, that would have made a great line in his final act because he had rehearsed it so many times in my write-ups.

Me not reacting was equally powerful. I wasn't biting by giving him an explosive reaction to his final coup de grace, but I did have a flash image of punching his cold callous face off his shoulders, kicking him in the rear end all the way out the school front door, and then beating the crap out of him in the parking lot!

This vision gave me an internal deviant happiness that was just a small spark in time, but I wanted it to last forever. I would have loved to see him run and hide like the coward he is when I delivered the first blow, but none of my reactions would have been proper, so I resisted.

With his stare, there was no difference between the color of his eyes and his pupil. There was a hollow look to him that did not indicate life. He had lowered the final axe, which symbolically chopped off my head to end the existence of an "enemy" in a space he wanted to control. It was finally over. He got what he worked so hard to achieve, and ironically, there was a sense of relief that came over me like I had somehow finally been relieved of his torture.

Freedom, yes finally, I thought but the reality of a new world in which I was about to enter from this professional fallout was only about to begin. I had no idea that more devastating reality lay ahead which would alter the course of my life further.

Unemployment benefits only covered half of my wages, so I immediately scrambled to figure out all the ways to reduce bills. After a careful evaluation of expenses, I noticed a trend in what I call "fear payments" such as short-term disability, long-term disability, cancer policies, and supplemental life. Why was I so fearful of all these things when I was healthy, and how stupid of me to unwisely spend so much money for these policies?

The sales pitch of being responsible and protecting your family, I fell for it hook, line, and sinker. My kids were all grown and on their own, so why did I waste my money on such frivolous stuff especially since now finding out all those plans were terminated in an instant. I spent so much money investing in these policies over the years and now it's all gone. Nothing to show for this "fear" investment. I wish they had offered "predatory boss insurance" now that I could have used.

How was I going to pay for my professional development to keep my school counseling certificate active and other expenses such as memberships in American Counseling Association, Kentucky Counseling Association, and National Board of Certified Counselors.

What about my student loan debt of $60K and the years of service for loan forgiveness by working in an eligible low-income school? I also could not finish my mental health counseling program either. I was screwed financially and had never dreamed I had burdened myself with so much debt? I had invested in myself and it felt selfish now.

Any of my possessions that had value were sold. I donated or gave away most of my belongings. Everything had become a burden to me and gave me no more pleasure. I had to move and didn't want to take anything with me. In the back of my mind, getting rid of everything felt like a good way to punish myself for such a failure in my life. I needed a consequence so I would never let this happen again.

A happy moment was giving my kids furniture and dishes along with miscellaneous items for their homes and making sure family heirlooms were given to the right person. I texted a copy of pictures to faraway friends who were happy to receive them. Doing all of this was therapeutic and made me feel good that I could give others something; however, my actions freaked my kids out because they thought I was acting like someone who was going to kill themselves.

There were many thoughts like that, especially during times of self-loathing, but I kept it a secret and fought urges that would come and go as I deepened into depression.

There was a panic that stirred inside from suddenly losing my livelihood. I guess what I am trying to express was that I was afraid of being homeless, and the thought was tapping at my feet daily. I don't want that to be my final landing place. I feel blessed that I have a home, but it is a burden to keep trying to rob Peter to pay Paul. There is no way I can keep it. I must sell before the bank gets wind that I'm unemployed.

Instinctively, I know I should be working but I'm broken inside and losing strength with the many hours of looking and applying for jobs. I had tried interviewing in the beginning because that is what people expected of me. My expressionless face and restraint in fighting tears said a lot to potential employers. Who wants to hire a school counselor that is so sad? I wouldn't hire me.

Interviewing in a school environment again had its own set of triggers. I trusted no one anymore not only in a school but in any employment situation for that matter. What if I landed in the same circumstances again? That would definitely throw me over the edge. It was not a risk worth taking, so I had to figure out something safer.

All I can think of every day was to inventory food, ration it out, not waste, only buy what I need, and alternate paying bills. I used to value my credit score but now could give a crap. I can't buy anything except food, so why do I need it? I am a "throwaway!" and I don't like living in this type of world.

I clearly know that most stores and restaurants are not accessible to me anymore. I check prices and make sure the register charges me correctly. I take things back that are not right or broken. I used to just eat the cost and not bother with returns. I used to buy things to make life easier; now I look around and see what I have that can be used for multiple purposes. I easily give up if there is something I need but don't have … it's okay.

Having fewer things makes me happier. It removes the complication of being a caretaker for stuff. That is way too much responsibility now and overwhelms the mind. Having nothing means nobody can take anything away from me. This is how I protect myself from further loss.

Throughout my career, I had saved a lot but it was mostly tied up in retirement money. So, after I blew through all my unemployment benefits and savings, I hit some of my retirement funds, and of course had to pay a hefty price in fines and taxes for early withdrawal. I justified this as my "rainy day" and needed the money yesterday. Unfortunately, I had to make the decision to take my teacher's retirement ten years early. It is not very much, but the urge to eat is so powerful that I didn't know any other choice. I did not want to go on any government assistance program.

I falsely acted like nothing has changed, but deep down I was extremely lost. I recognized I'm not whole, but my family wants me back the way I was before the predator crossed my path. I desperately want that too but as I search for "back" it appears so far off in the distance now and unreachable.

I longed for someone to protect me, but I could never ask for help because then I will be owned again. The predator had owned me without my permission, and I will never let anyone have that prize again. I'd rather face the fear of living in my car, so I can be free.

It used to be long ago that people only moved when there was a new job opportunity, transfer, or to be with family. Now families are leaving because they are forced. It doesn't feel good when you are forced to leave a community you thought you were part of and gave you a sense of belonging.

Now that I have been fired, I desperately yearn to return home where I was born and so have visited California in the hopes there is some place I can afford. I did not recognize my old neighborhood as the signs on the businesses are not in English anymore. They are a foreign language and I don't know how to read them. That explains why the job openings request bilingual applicants only.

I think of my students and how housing changes affected them. How can they bond to a school community when they are constantly on the move?

Some of these kids moved so much their cumulative folder never caught up with them. Having shelter is a basic human need, and when it is threatened, removed, or out of reach, our school families cannot plant themselves or become a stable part of a community which everyone desires.

Middle-class people who accepted the American dream of being independent and suddenly find themselves closer to homelessness have difficulty asking for a place to lay their head. It is our culture of independence that gets in the way of either accepting or asking for this type of help. It feels like another failure at a most inopportune time. No one wants to give up their independence, especially since so much cultural value was put on it throughout the life span.

As I drift around dragging my roots, I long for a community which I can call home again. I don't know if I ever will be confident to risk "planting" myself, but it is something I so much desire yet cannot find the courage to throw out my anchor.

Rambling, rambling, rambling this is what I've been doing now because not securing housing has heightened my anxiety immensely. This level of uncertainty rises each day and has given me intense fear of landing in the street.

CHAPTER 27:
CURRENCY FOR THE POOR

Losing my income quickly made me aware of how desperate I was to just have food and keep a roof over my head. It is amazing how fast I went from comfortably supporting myself to falling in a desperate fight for survival.

The sudden loss of lifestyle forced me to truly understand what Maslow's hierarchy of needs meant because I could not focus on anything else until I secured food, shelter, medicine, and at least a minimum basic standard of living.

There was no prior experience applying for government programs in my background nor was anyone in my family a specialist in that area. I probably would not seek their advice anyway because pride and embarrassment would get in the way. I also never paid attention to the politics of assistance programs because they were for other people who needed help, not me.

A graduate degree was not going to help me with understanding the paperwork process. I did my best to navigate the complicated forms for seeking much-needed resources thinking it would only be temporary. There are so many hoops to jump through, and I needed immediate help now not later after the lengthy approval process was obtained.

Applying for government assistance was a demeaning feeling like I was just being harassed as a way to stay alive. But the reality is I was desperate and willing to take the harassment in order to buy food. I had to suck it up no matter how asinine I thought the process was because I couldn't change it anyway.

In my mind, assistance was a last resort and served as a constant reminder of the failing situation that I found myself now navigating. I basically was surrendering to the idea I could not fully take care of myself. How devastating!

The government will accept your failure and teach you a lesson by owning your behavior because you obviously have no control over it anyway.

I have such disdain for anyone owning me let alone an agency, but I humbly need to eat. I became consumed with securing food and tried to think of creative ways to obtain this necessary evil without presenting myself to family that I was hungry.

Although official government workers appear very helpful, they know they have the power to take away, give, or pawn off on another worker your case decisions. You are at the mercy of your own attitude in getting the most help.

It took a while for me to have approval for medical assistance, and food help came through with a whopping budget of $16 a month. I declined the food offer but was very thankful of the medical coverage. Unfortunately, I had no idea of the continued hoops I would be asked to jump through just to maintain being eligible for medical coverage. I pondered not being insured at all but quickly realized that having a chronic medical condition with on again off again insurance was interfering with successful treatment.

I had been starting and stopping medication based on no insurance, Obamacare, and Medicaid insurance coverage coming and going. I was in a "damn if you do, damn if you don't" system. My medical condition had deteriorated from medical neglect and now was interfering with my ability to work.

If I could have just been able to stabilize my condition, along with housing and food, it could allow me back in the workforce where hopefully I could obtain my own private insurance. This of course was a wish on my part but not possible under assistance.

I needed some fast cash to offset my expenses for food and shelter.

Cash is income that cannot be traced, and I would be willing to not claim it just so I could maintain having medical care or buy food. I was that desperate. I was on the edge of making too much money from my small retirement even though I couldn't afford to pay bills or buy enough food. I had to report every income source I had, and if anyone lived in the household with me, their information had to be given too.

We are living in the digital age where every financial transaction is recorded, so it's hard to not declare something as income. Cash cannot be tracked. Cash would help me buy the necessities I need and keep the bill collectors away. Cash would not interfere with receiving the minimal government assistance I qualified for because it can't be traced, and I would not have to claim the income that would knock me out of qualifying. I would be willing to break the law to have basic human needs met. This is what desperate people do who have no previous history of violations and don't have a network to help navigate the system. This is why middle-class people fail so quickly during job loss and go straight to homelessness. They are not used to asking for help nor do they know even what's available.

What employed people don't realize is that an unemployed person can't think of even obtaining employment until they figure out how to exist for the day. It is a vicious cycle because if they were employed, they wouldn't have to figure out how to survive the day. An unemployed brain goes into an anxious need for survival, which includes food and shelter and in my case medicine too. Until these needs are met, nothing else matters and the future is not even considered in decision-making.

To add insult to injury, a person can take a lesser-paying job with no problem, but they will immediately be removed from receiving benefits that will help them get back on their feet. The need to survive is still in force, and the increased expenses from working such as transportation, gas, clothing, and food becomes overwhelming. This is like constantly having the carrot stick moved knowing you will never reach it.

Because of these barriers, the dependency on government assistance gets reinforced through this dysfunctional part of helping our citizens recover as they hold out for a higher-paying job to fully meet their needs.

I thought of different ways to obtain cash without being tracked and realized there really is not a lot of opportunities that are legal. I could now see why drug dealing is a risk worth taking for those who are needing cash to survive, but I wasn't going to engage in that because I still had some standards for myself.

When I was working at my low-income school, there was a pattern of behavior I didn't understand at the time but noticed and just kept it logged in the back of my mind.

Some of my female parents who were trying their best to make ends meet would eventually become addicted to drugs. They didn't start out that way because I had known them as a family for several years, and they seemed engaged with their children and the school.

A divorce or separation had changed their situation, and the first clue I noticed of a desperate act was at the end of the school day during dismissal. When the mom would come to pick up their child, I would open the passenger door to board the student and I noticed the inside door panels were removed.

This was how drugs were hidden for transport to another destination. This was an easy way for moms in our school to make cash. These were good women who had a heart of gold for their child and now they were desperate to earn money that couldn't be traced nor interfere with their government assistance.

Eventually, my good moms would not stop at transporting drugs, and they would become addicted themselves or placed in a situation of violence. Their children who previously didn't have any academic or emotional issues would start to show signs of anxiety and worry for their parent.

What if our government would allow employers like fast food restaurants in a low-income area to pay their employees with cash and it would not have to be reported if under a certain amount? This would give low-income individuals a way to earn money through work and help make ends meet without turning to an illegal way of earning cash.

I can't imagine how different it would be for my students if this legal route of cash earning was available to their parent. I think employers that are designated in these low-income areas should also receive tax breaks for their business being in a designated "green zone." This would be a win for employees, employers, and the children in the community. Also, it's a great first job for youth who need to earn cash and gain valuable customer service experience. Cash would make these types of jobs competitive, and a worker would more than likely make every effort to keep their position.

Another way to earn cash is to barter with stolen guns. Big cash can be made this way and that's why we see so many teenagers shoot at each other and commit crimes. Possessing a stolen weapon and firing the trigger can become words for a desperate person who has failed to develop problem-solving and impulse control skills.

Crime amongst youth and low-income families is a problem that will not be resolved until we satisfy their physiological needs first. Allowing cash to be made through legal means by working and gaining skill would help kids contribute to their families.

Drugs, guns, and cash have become the currency for low-income individuals and families trying to make ends meet. There should be a better way to legally earn cash without being penalized by government assistance programs so one can eventually reach equilibrium and get back on their feet.

CHAPTER 28:
GET OUT AND TAKE ANOTHER JOB

The economy is doing fantastic. The jobs report shows unemployment at its lowest. In the news, our mayor states frequently how he is bringing new business to our area and with it arrive thousands of jobs.

This is an important statistic because he can claim credit in recruiting new employers and jobs under his leadership. This is especially announced during reelection time. What he fails to tell you is that most of the livable wage paying positions are already filled by out-of-state employees who are relocating with the company to our area.

Statements about job growth by politicians are so positive for the citizens and deliver a message that everyone should be doing well; therefore, there are jobs available if you want them.

To add to the inflated figures, there are thousands of job openings listed on employment websites for each city. A lot of these listings are continuously advertised so an employer can keep a fresh resume pool in the event a position becomes available in the future.

Recruiters also need to complete their main job task of interviewing potential candidates even though no opening exists. You can be called simply to do an interview, but they are not required to disclose if an actual job opening exists.

Unfortunately, in our area toxic politicians will look at the total number of job listings on employment websites and claim them as a real number when stating how many positions are available in their community. They also ignore the fact that a lot of openings are continuously reposted which inflates the numbers as well.

These tactics are not only misleading but become incredibly discouraging to someone who is unemployed and spends numerous hours applying for jobs that really aren't available. The constant rejection contributes to the cycle of unemployment to poverty when applicants are unsuccessful in finding work to sustain their basic human needs in a timely manner.

Seeking a school counselor position is best done by having solid network connections with the hiring school. Most importantly having a good reference from the school principal who knows my work and can easily describe my strengths as a team member would play a huge role in the hiring decision.

Unfortunately, the principal was not an option for me to use as a reference. It would be like asking my former abusive husband for his blessing in allowing me to marry another man.

Not having this preferred reference that most school employers require was a huge red flag on how they considered me for potential employment. Interview after interview always led to questions pertaining to my principal/counselor relationship and how we worked as a team.

It felt like a vacuum had sucked the remaining life out of me, as emotional doom overwhelmed my entire body during this part of the interview because even after the loss of my job, I still had to protect the predator and carefully watch my words. It was quite difficult to think of or describe examples of work that would be normal for potential employers to hear. The pain of the relationship was so pervasive that it wiped out "normal" and so I nervously froze momentarily searching my mind for a quick answer that would satisfy the interviewer.

It is a known fact that you should never talk negative about your boss in an interview, so the thought that I still had to defend him made me want to throw up. I had not planned how any aspect of my life would be after leaving the clutches of that predator, so I was blindsided by still having this horrible nightmare following me.

Any gasp of life I had left was sucked out as I became deflated during the interview process, knowing how much power and control he still had over me even though I was no longer under his employ.

The routine questioning on the school positions made me realize something emotionally was very wrong with me. I had lost passion and excitement of being in a school setting. The environment had a dark appearance that once was so full of light. I didn't want to look at the students in the hallway as I walked to the interview site. I wasn't going to let my love for school counseling become unleashed like I had previously. I had been too emotionally attached to my students and their families and that wasn't going to happen again because when they are suddenly ripped away from you, the pain is immeasurable.

There was no way I could trust any of the staff at these schools. Their smiles appeared diabolical to me even if the intent was genuine. I had seen that behavior from those who attacked. What if they were like them?

There was no energy left in my being or desire to fend off another secret school culture. I trusted no one even though I didn't know these people or even have a conversation with them during the interview. A simple smile which everyone uses to greet was now viewed by me as deviate with some sort of motive to manipulate and destroy.

These interviews also required talking about data and the importance it had on a student's education. As I listened to the interviewer's questions, I thought to myself, "Yes, I too once believed in data and it was all a lie!" I couldn't honestly answer their question because I would have to expose an injustice played against children, so I would ramble some generic response that educators like to hear, then emotionally drift off from the interview.

My brain was filled with flashbacks of so many meetings I had with parents where I discussed their child's data and growth and believed the information was accurate and representative. I had tremendous guilt flood me during the interview as I realized I had been part of the deception the moment I unknowingly gave false data to the parent.

It was hard to know where I fit anymore or what direction to pursue for employment. I had great difficulty seeking advice from those in my circle, as being unemployed was not something they had dealt with since their teens. I was like a deer in the headlights not knowing which move would save my life.

Stagnation became easier, but it kept me from facing reality, and because I was not reemployed under "society's" timeline, destructive remarks blurted freely to encourage me to find any job. I had to endure statements of "just get over it or we have all had bad bosses." It is followed by a caring chuckle, so I guess the words shouldn't be hurtful.

There was so much power in those dismissive statements that erupted deep anger and sadness inside of me. I know that is not what others had in mind when they delivered their best motivating technique, but my already depressive feelings have me secretly holding a gun and these words become my bullets. I would fight self-deprecating behavior for days after the remarks and became nonproductive and catatonic until I could lift the spell.

My story had become more minimized with each exposure, and the consequences of my divulging were endlessly listening to another person's "bad boss" stories. Our experiences were the same in their mind. "I was annihilated and you still exist, so how is that the same?" I wanted to scream it to their face.

If I had been physically abused by my boss and his gang, they would be more caring, but because the wounds were from daggers of hatred that pierced my skin and were forever buried in my body, they can't possibly exist. I feel forced to conceal the etchings of my internal pain once again to my pile of stacked-up trauma.

In the beginning of unemployment, family and friends were very helpful and offered job leads to positions that were quite different from my employment history. They acknowledged it wasn't something they would take but it's a job.

I had to desperately fix what I had broken, so my mind was focused on finding what I had lost. I could not see myself being one more day miserable in a job I did not like nor go to school to become. Unfortunately, I offended the person who gave me a lead because I did not pursue their effort.

It is not because I was too good to take the job; it's because emotionally, I was in a dysfunctional thought process of replacing comparably what had been lost, and this fixation is hidden from the helping party. It was a matter of emotional timing with me because after an extended period when much processing had occurred, the same offer probably would have been accepted. This bridge was burned by then because of my inaction, so no other opportunities will come from this helper.

When I presented myself to the unemployment office, there was a group of us attending orientation and the person in charge gave us a "good talking" too about how we are in this unfortunate situation because of our failure to do something right at the company who terminated our employment.

We were encouraged to fix our poor work ethics by working harder, be on time, show up every day, be a team player! "I did that and more and look how it worked out for me," I thought to myself.

I felt like a prisoner who was trying to claim "I'm innocent!" It didn't matter what I thought because the end result was the fact, I had lost my job, will never return to my school, and had my 413 students were ripped from my care. The grief was overwhelming and no one wanted to hear my personal story of such loss.

The unemployment office offered retraining courses, and we had to act quickly or it was off the table. They provided two choices for a new career: medical coder or truck driver. I didn't want either one of these, as they sounded so boring and I belonged in the helping field; however, I felt I had an ace in the hole that may help me with my predicament.

I had made an appointment with the unemployment counselor, and since it was away from the group, I thought she would understand my situation better if I plead my case privately. I explained to her that during my employment, I had been working on obtaining my second master's degree in mental health counseling and all I needed was my practicum and internship.

The coursework had been completed, and the cost was the same as training me to become a truck driver or medical coder. Would the unemployment office pay my tuition to complete the degree, so I could continue helping children? The answer without even consideration was absolutely "NO!" She stated I had too much education and they were not going to invest in more graduate classes, only training courses in truck driver or medical coder. She further elaborated those training courses are no longer available because I had missed my window of opportunity during orientation.

Where do I fit now? Here I remain in a neutral position trying to get one foot out from the predator and putting the other into seeking a new direction that I did not choose. These two worlds have me frozen in a constant state of anxiety and uncertainty. I really want to run away because that feels like a good choice to protect me from the hostile world.

As time passed, thoughts of my students would inspire a hidden answer to my desperation that had been there all along. In fact, it was reflecting back on career guidance lessons with the kids, where we talked about the type of lifestyle we wanted to live and making it a significant part of decision-making towards career choice. I don't know why I had not made the connection to my own life because it sure would have helped me sooner and not allowed so much pressure and misery to build up in trying to think of the right answer for my next job.

A career should be something that allows me to enjoy the type of lifestyle I choose. Pursuing that direction first instead of putting emphasis on one single career choice for life is far more protective than putting all my eggs in one basket and hoping for the best rewarding job.

Life is so unexpected, change is constant, and the nature of people who can become my boss is unpredictable, so focusing on "lifestyle" instead of the career I had lost reframed my attitude and broke the barrier that kept me stagnant.

This new strategy just might allow free pursuit of any type of job that will work as long as it contributes to obtaining the lifestyle dream. Lord, I hope I'm not lying to myself.

CHAPTER 29:
PURPOSE AND HOPE

Hatred annihilates equilibrium of the soul. The oscillation of its effect discards many talented individuals who may never know their full potential when they become lost through victimization. There is no rhyme nor reason for its justification. The hater's fuel can only be explained as a self-serving grip that clinches on to good people who did not deserve its wrath.

Losing my job at the hands of hatred was a destructive force that collaterally damaged my worldview, disintegrated any thoughts of purpose, and quashed all chances of hope rising. The hatred had been so much in my face that it recalculated who I was. It felt like my pilot light had been extinguished and all the synergistic parts of life were no longer connected to keep my emotional health positively functioning.

Thinking about the loss consumed my dimmed energy at every waking moment. I had never realized being me until another person had challenged my existence and determined my worth. I plunged into this grief. It's like you finally see yourself as a "being" and realize it's for real. It reminds me when I was a kid and saw my shadow for the first time and learned it was a reflection of my existence.

Purpose and hope inflated my body and the piercing of losing my career deflated any opportunity for a future. My response was to cry and continue to cry until I fell into a mental black hole. The space around me was so empty. There was no color, no people or things. I had emotionally flatlined. I was alone … so very alone.

My mind was lost in searching for "purpose" and "hope." This special nourishment that once was so plentiful had now become barren. The feeling of searching turned to anxiousness as I became withdrawn and wanted to stay in the safety of my home alone, but I soon feared the walls were closing in and I wanted to run.

Without a purpose, how can I justify my existence? I had failed and now was wandering in a life of self-pity because I believed I had done everything right that was asked of me and this didn't work. How can I have hope?

Living by the rules of success our parents teach us, like work hard, be honest, do what's right and life will be good. These rules had guided me and now I believe were all a lie when the predator turned my worldview upside down.

How could I have been deceived from these rules? I had found extreme fault in my thinking. My worldview was wrong. It took a sociopath in an elementary school to challenge my belief system.

I lost confidence in my ability to know the right direction to pursue because wrong is so threatening and highlights my ignorance on how unfair life truly is if you are not well rounded. I questioned myself as a mom and felt guilty for teaching my children about these same rules that were passed down from my parents. When you have an encounter with a predator who targets you, there needs to be an addendum but that won't make sense until you are violated.

A sociopath thinks so differently. I had no experience, knowledge, or training on how to diffuse such a charming, manipulative, and ill person that only knows hate. I had come to believe now that I deserved for this predator to treat me the way he did. He earned my purpose and hope because they were artificial. I had not protected them fully.

Had I truly been a good counselor, I would have known his evil ways and I would have been able to keep my job. I lied to myself about my abilities and reflected back on why no one else in my school would step forward. I had no representation on my merits, so it made it easy to believe he was right in targeting me.

These self-deprecating thoughts were overwhelming and were drawing me to end my life. I had no purpose nor plan to fix my situation or self. I cried uncontrollably and alone so no one would know my pain. I could not share it because I couldn't understand its meaning.

My time of despair would happen so frequently as I was walking further and further away from living. Being a target had exposed me to uncovering how ugly the world was now as I look at life through an evil lens. I had allowed the predator to steal my purpose and totally digest any hope. I handed him a delicious win because I could not find any worth in myself.

CHAPTER 30:
SUICIDE

Suicide is a very personal subject that I find hard to talk about and would never discuss this feeling to anyone. I don't want it misunderstood for seeking sympathy nor do I want a reaction to change my mind. What I did seek was a safe place to actually say I had these very strong thoughts and they were occupying a lot of space in my heart. I also didn't want to take this route but it was something that was so intrusive and kept invading my mind daily. I wanted these thoughts to go away just like the predator.

I really feel this invasion was a haunt in my mind that came out of the bowels of the dark world I had been drowning in for the last year. It was hard to grasp the direct hatred that someone had towards me that I had never met before. Where does such an idea come from in a human being that can justify motivation for annihilating someone without conscience. This was such a barrier to comprehend, understand, and except. It felt like this was the new perception my worldview was forced to accept because the behaviors were so highly rewarded. I wanted no part of this type of world.

It seemed everyone had accepted my situation as being blown out of proportion, and there is no need to elaborate further on what happened. They got the idea; they got the gist of it. It simply had run its course and became a broken record so no further need talking about it. My issue was resolved with everyone but me.

I knew the predator was going about life like nothing had changed, and I was going about life like everything was different and there was no familiarity or calm. I didn't have anything to look forward to anymore. I felt a need to accept that I had accomplished everything I was supposed to do and my plan for life had been completed. I felt justified by recognizing that I had enjoyed a good life up until my encounter with the predator and my time on earth had come to the end of living.

Physically and emotionally, I could not feel anymore. My crying body had become routine, and I quit noticing. The pleasures I had known were gone, and I was walking through life simply doing the motions. I hated seeing myself in photos because I saw nothing but misery, and I wept for the person who was lost in the picture. It wasn't me because there was no life in my eyes like it used to be.

My story was never validated, so it is another thing I'm told in life to ignore because it really didn't happen. Why are emotional wounds so complicated and hard for others to see? I have been patronized by so many and no longer feel legitimate.

I arrived at the threshold of being satisfied with my life and dying wasn't a fear. I felt like a baseball player that had stayed in the game too long and didn't retire before he lost his edge. I tried feverishly to wipe my last year of counseling from my mind so I could falsely create a positive image that I left at the top of my game. I was only lying to myself of course because the truth eventually would flood my thoughts and remind me of the miserable last year of my profession.

The haunts were becoming stronger and more intense as the belief that I had no right to earn a living was reinforced in my mind. This was a privilege for the few who had power. How could I even take care of myself anymore when basic human needs which were once routine now are hard to obtain as a portion? Self-harm thinking had become so common in my daily life that it felt like a "creeper" waiting in the lurks. I never knew when it would show itself and dare me to act on their pleasure.

One day I had wandered into my garage seeking I don't know what, but the vivid thought of what I should do to solve my numbness came to me as an evil plan in seconds just like the plan to kill the predator. I can't say that it was an impulsive feeling I had because bits and pieces of thoughts had been there for a while and now had accumulated like a malignant tumor from each miserable day that had passed.

I had lost my confidence as a counselor, lost my friends, lost my 413 students, and most of all, it was very disheartening knowing that my loved ones could not understand why I was in such a severe state of grief.

My expectation from family and friends was to understand my grief. I had emotionally died and it felt so permanent. No words, no pep talk, no nothing was going to resuscitate me, only sincere validation of my story and understanding what I was going through. I wanted interpretation of what happened. I wanted why. I wanted everything that loved ones could not offer because they had no experience with the destructive mindset of a habitual hater. I failed to recognize this key understanding would be the catalyst for helping; unfortunately, I misinterpreted their emotional disconnect as not caring and that they had lost respect for me.

Holding back my story felt physically like I had a severed arm and no one would approach to help stop the bleeding because they could not see the blood. My identity as a school counselor was gone. My purpose as a mom felt over. I had no place anymore.

Emotionally, I had arrived at the edge of a cliff and when looking down, there was no bottom. I had no personal goals nor long-term plans. How did my mind become so blank and black without color? It was as if I could actually see inside my skull and there was nothing there to guide me. My mind used to be full of ideas constantly across a gamut of domains and now when I look out, I see an abyss.

When I walked into the garage, I had been crying all day as usual. I really loved my old car because it had the most fantastic sound system. It was paid for, so nobody could take it away from me. It was strange the way I looked at it now as I stared towards the driver's seat and pictured myself fixating. This image was real, intense, and disturbing. I hate that I have these images in my head and they pop in so easily now.

I briefly thought of my kids and justified they were doing great on their own as young adults. Later I would realize this snapshot of their well-being was so imperfect because at the time, I never considered how my actions would have affected them if I had been successful at terminating my life. I never thought of the aftermath, only the immediate moments of before the act and they were doing just fine. How did someone like me who was a planner come to be a person who can't even look past the moment?

As I stood in my closed garage touching the rear of the car, I looked down and had noticed that my dog followed me. He was looking up periodically and investigating the garage floor. He had no idea what I was planning in my head. He once again was acting loyal to me as he stood by my side. I didn't deserve his faithfulness but his presence had a jarring effect.

We stared at one another as if a silent dialog was happening between us. He pierced my heart with his sweet eyes to hook me from selfishness, and his persistent concerned look at me was a direct notice we were connecting and once again he was unconditionally delivering loyalty.

My four-legged friend was the one who comforted me when I divorced, he was the one who filled my empty heart when my children left for college, and he was the one who kept me warm when I couldn't afford heat in my home during grad school days.

It was my selfishness that placed my own personal burdens on my dog without thought. He never swayed from his loyalty as a pet to comfort his owner in need. What a "wake-up to reality" his stare engrained in me. He had all the power without giving conditions nor saying a word. He felt my heartache through his eyes and carried my emotional burden on his back. I had been searching since my job loss for purpose in life because that was how I defined myself, and for some reason looking at my dog simplified things and put it in perspective. I had to ask myself why am I being so complicated?

Why was having a purpose so powerful in sustaining existence? What ridiculous nonproductive pressure to place on a person who is badly emotionally wounded and not clear in thoughts. I was exhausted with the effort it took to merely exist let alone define the direction I needed to go.

My life was drastically changed, so I needed to stop my ordinary thinking because the old guidelines I set for myself were not working for a long time. After deep contemplation, a glimmer of thought came to mind. What if I gave myself permission to accept life without a purpose for now? What would happen if I put purpose on hold?

I had been relying on others for rightful validation of my story and the intense pain it caused me. I had been relying on direction and rescuing from others. I had been shutting out life until these intense needs were met. Because of this, I had handed over my recovery to others and they too came to own me.

My moment with my dog had given me a gift, as it briefly stopped all the noise of my complicated dreadful life. I found there was a part of me still inside that the predator had not touched. I could help me. I could depend on me. I could give me exactly what I needed.

I gave myself permission to idle, reflect, and explore a new life without time constraints or well-meaning influence from others. I allowed distance from my negative world by investing emotionally in myself. This gave a calming peace for the first time as I accepted this new deal.

Designating these intense feelings in my life as "my depression time" and stating it would soon be solved because it is now a protected "time-out" allowed me to embrace being alone without feeling loneliness because I would busy working on me.

If I was going to be whole, I needed to completely process what had happened and seek answers that would satisfy me instead of seeking validation from others. Being open for new business allowed me to work on solving the mystery that had taken over my life and ignited a new journey towards healing. It's about time for me to relearn living.

CHAPTER 31:
FAILURE

"Success is not final and failure is not fatal ... it is the courage to continue that counts!"~**Winston Churchill**

The "purest" form of failure is through my own effort and doing my best but still failing. I'm completely in charge of that destiny. What I experienced with the predator was the most complex "contaminated failure" because no amount of effort on my part was ever considered.

It was part of his playbook that targets must yield and accept their demise so he can cleanse the area they occupy. The students and I were a mere contaminate in a space he wanted to control. It was most unfortunate we had been in the right place at the wrong time. Because of his power, he was in charge of our destiny and none of us had a say.

Self-loathing would require me to spend every waking moment analyzing and re-analyzing in my head what I could have done differently. I could have been more attentive to the needs of teachers and stronger on building alliances that possibly could have protected me. I played the "could've, should've, would've" drama in my head and that was as useless as believing that I could actually have stopped the predator from his attack.

What personally made this downfall so devastating is the fact that my worldview had been challenged, altered, and redefined to include a sinister element. I had been viewing the world from an incomplete perspective. The predator allowed me to completely understand evil people can be anywhere even in places you least expect, like an elementary school. It is difficult to protect yourself from their assault unless you are highly skilled in understanding clinically significant personality deficits that are connected to narcissistic functioning.

My professional failure continued to deepen with the thought of leaving my students in the hands of a principal who didn't care whether they succeeded or were academically crushed. His lack of conscience easily numbed him from the difficult future that lay ahead for them as a result of his actions. I also had great concern for the type of like-minded school counselor he was bringing on board as my replacement.

Reluctantly, I would have to reconcile the losses and surrender to the toxic environment that had been the norm for our district but now was going to be much more elevated and diabolical. This acknowledgement came with diminished hope of simply "riding it out."

Conceding notified me that I had become a member of a small club of people who have ever experienced the wrath of such hatred. The "untouched" good people had drifted away and could not see the menacing phantom who was single-handedly picking targets. Our school had an illness that was not going to be cured.

It was hard for me to accept finality, as publicly and privately I was so humiliated and filled with intense feelings of failure. I had abandoned students who had real mental health issues and needed help. Their parents lost trust as they perceived I wouldn't return their calls or emails. Teachers had joined the frenzy by also believing I had abandoned my post. Even my own children thought this failure was something I could fix. My extended family had believed the rumors that were spread in our small town about my firing but never had the courage to ask me what happened.

I had lost trust in my school friendships, as their need for survival outweighed the complicated problem of exposing dirt in our school system. They were dedicated to hold the secret and keep business as usual like I had learned to do in childhood.

Even the unemployment office informed me that my job loss was due to my own fault and that I needed to change careers. They further elaborated I had not shown success in maintaining employment in such a specialty area.

Shelter insecurity heightened my anxiety, as my mortgage company stated they would not approve any future home loans if I hadn't changed my profession. Every aspect of my life was affected by this unfortunate encounter with the predator.

The more I scrambled for understanding what was lost, the more he claimed my soul. He was like a tornado spinning me by my feet and making sure I wiped out every aspect of my life.

As an adult, how did I become so unprepared to handle an assault from such a person? He infested me with an unfamiliar failure that made recovery seem unachievable. I was lost for appropriate coping skills at such a complicated level.

I grievously understood that I had chosen the wrong approach when trying to protect myself from the attack by engaging from a "defensive stance." This is why I had so many deep wounds. The more he attacked, the deeper he dug into unprocessed trauma from my life. I wish I had more courage directly to call him out to his face. I was not that brave because it is disrespectful to challenge someone of authority. This was a childhood rule I learned. It took this assault for me to realize you should never give respect to someone who disrespects you. They are not worthy if they can't honor you as a human being.

Physically he was a man but socially he was a boy, so I had failed to under-stand he had characteristics like all school bullies, such as being a coward and easily have his feelings hurt. The hatred protected his vulnerability and became the gatekeeper to keeping his secret. His unthreading would have happened had I delivered a public blow that was wide in scope and deep in authority, but because I had a weakness in believing so many of my own childhood rules, I reserved doing something that was way out of charac-ter for me. It is weird to think that I too had a commonality with him, as my defense came from my childhood and his behavior came from the same era.

At the time, I didn't grasp the magnitude of evil only understanding evil and that was his language level. The only vocabulary he would comprehend was if I projected his hatred right back at him publicly. My punishment would have been revenge, but the truth would have been revealed or at least questioned by others. I wanted to be the bigger person more than lowering myself to treating someone so inappropriately.

What I didn't consider was the fact he had no empathy, so my maltreat-ment would not affect him the same as it would a regular human being. He would have reacted by puffing up and going to a full-blown uncontrol-lable temper tantrum, since my action would have publicly threatened his grandiose idea of self, and then I would just receive another write-up of insubordination in my file.

Sadly, I failed to deliver this precise blow to his core and that was my biggest regret that I needed to get past. Never again will I be so cowardice because the rules of conflict resolution do not apply to someone with pathologi-cal traits. I should have delivered a direct hit to his cowardice soul right from the git-go. Unfortunately, I would have blamed myself for thinking my behavior lost my job, but in actuality, my job was lost the moment he targeted me.

I finally understood why he adopted hate to guide his moral compass because it easily allowed disconnect and gave a distorted belief that his attack wasn't personal. Because he had deficits in emotional attachment, people were mere objects, even children. There was no differentiating for targeting; we all fit the same.

Hatred requires no critical thinking skills or possession of individual talent, and it certainly does not include participating in good works for mankind. It is simply an easy catalyst for extinguishing threats that obsessively roll around in the mind of a predator.

Understanding and accepting hatred's contribution to my unintended failure did not relieve my grief overnight, but it tremendously helped in unthreading the spectrum differences between the predator's belief system and my own.

Taking that first step towards understanding would involve breaking into my own self-discovery and using it as emotional protection, while I allowed a backdoor perspective of analyzing his pathology and understanding the imaginary world in which he lived. As painful as it was, I had to take responsibility for my emotional behavior if I wanted to sever the tether that was still binding me to the predator.

I was capable of understanding the power of that move, as it would put me in the driver's seat. The separation will help me realize the predator cannot have ownership of his behavior because it is flawless and needs no improvement in his mind; therefore, he will always remain a passenger that never unlocked real control of himself. He will always be driven by others.

I cannot blame myself nor the predator for my wounded outcome, but instead learning such a complicated personality deficit has given me enlightenment from a different perspective that allows a glimmer of clarity towards recovery. This was the beginning of severing the toxic relationship that was still binding us together because up until that time, his presence was still in my mind.

Enormous emotional harm resulted from so many areas of my life affected. I can't undo all the feelings just because the assault wasn't personal to him in his mind. The justification of his disconnect did not match the damage from the grenade he threw on my existence. How can I not take it personally when the attack systemically affected my entire life?

My failure was devastating and his failure was rewarding. I guess in his simple mind the difference was just a matter of interpretation. He adamantly saw his perception as the right one because he could continue enjoying life uninterrupted.

My gift and curse at the same time was possession of an empathetic response and so I do not have the capacity like the predator to automatically disconnect. Viewing the value of life from different perspectives is why our stories cannot have the same personal meaning. Even though there was only one plan in which we were all involved, the outcome was two different stories. Normal and pathological circumstances are two parallel lines which can never intersect because they are foreign to one another. My line was all that mattered to me, and this is where the answer to peace would lie.

Delving through the dark side of both the predator and my personal history, was such an extremely painful journey that finally unlocked answers to emotional baggage which had burden me without resolve. I am so proud of the progress made in processing its meaning instead of burying trauma like in the past. It is amazing how a suffocating cloud was lifted from my soul as I found peace through my own actions. The predator unknowingly had helped me resolve past emotional injuries that had stacked up over the years as a result of our paths crossing.

Shedding emotional burdens that had been engrained with who I thought I was gave me a new freedom, as it lifted depression from my soul and allowed me to go exactly where I wanted to be instead of hoping where I should have been.

I truly had been set free through taking control over my own well-being, and this discovery wiped thoughts of no hope, no future, and no goals. The new opening created allowed ideas to once again gently pour through my existence. It felt like someone had just put new batteries in me to restore my life.

CHAPTER 32:
FORGIVENESS

For a long time, I had many intrusive thoughts of killing the predator because I strongly believed his heartless soul did not deserve to be on the face of this earth. Even after my firing, these visions haunted my mind daily and were a constant reminder of evil. I hated it that he still had power over me.

Flashbacks of graphic images showing his demise would bring me satisfaction for the moment. I had no remorse in my thought, as I felt justified because of his violations. Thoughts were just thoughts; how harmful could they be? It wasn't like I was ever going to act on them.

I also couldn't stop thinking of his accomplices. The faces of these afflicted people who were under his "cult spell" would pop in my mind, as their misdeeds reminded me their role was just as evil. I wanted his gang of thugs to feel intense professional humiliation as fallen soldiers who would be forced to retreat their miserable life back to being alone, defeated, and knowing only failure.

Throughout the school year, I had felt mixed emotions over my attitude towards colleagues and witnesses who distanced themselves from me. Wrestling this byproduct of the fallout gave me deep sadness, as they were my friends and collaborators. We were a team who shared a commonality of advocating for our students and delivering the best ideas and direction for their outcome. They had felt my liability and decided to go on without me. I grieve the loss of our camaraderie.

Their lack of action felt like I was thrown on a desolate island with sharks in a feeding frenzy all around. I could see them, hear their voices, and watch them move past me as we separated our friendship, and they fled on a life raft together. I understood the unwritten message there was no room for me to share their platform.

In the end, I protected myself by believing their presence was artificial because they had no idea of the sadness I felt in the loss of our friendship and most of all the simultaneous severing of my membership in the school community.

Internally, I felt betrayal from the school family and didn't know how to make sense of my feelings. We all knew it was a permanent parting, but to lose so many friends at once was overwhelming and tore at my heart.

For a long time, I wanted my colleagues to experience just at least a portion of the hell of being a target so they would understand the deepest pain of what it meant when they left me, but I really wouldn't want to wish any part of that devious violation on anybody.

How can I cleanse myself of all this toxicity that penetrated deep inside and raveled around my brain? My body had become broken and my face apathetic. My legs had only taken me through motion as my arms dangled with no life. I look at the ground and it is a safe place, as I don't want to see what is around me. I don't want to know what's coming my way; I just accept that it will.

In the back of my mind, I know forgiving is a good solution for moving through a trauma, but how can I get past the fact that someone must pay? I found it hard to even consider forgiving when there were so many significant areas of my life affected by these haters. Each one is a crime and each one is deserving of accountability. How can I break it down and pulverize the dreadful experience to find something positive like forgiving?

When I least expected it, the answers would come to me one dreadful night when I lost control of my car at high speed. Four months prior, I had been trying to obtain a referral to my cardiologist because a prescribed long-term medication was causing drastic dips in blood pressure. Unfortunately, I was new to Medicaid and the nurse practitioner assigned as my primary care said she would handle taking over prescribing so ordered a refill without seeing me for my condition. No referral to my former cardiologist was necessary because a Medicaid provider knows how to keep costs down.

On the long drive home, I had a couple of dizzy spells indicating my blood pressure was very low. I thought I could fight off the symptom like I had so many times before and besides that, I was almost home. This time it was somewhat different; it was late at night and I was extremely tired on top of it from my busy day spending with my daughter. Without realizing, I drifted into the gravel portion of the shoulder and the drop off made it difficult to return to the road. My second attempt would end in disaster, as I had overcorrected.

The steering wheel spun uncontrollably dislodging my grip and flailing my arms in the air. My car began to rapidly spin in a circle but it felt like slow motion giving me time to know something bad might happen. The force of the speed propelled me to the other side of the highway.

I feared being hit from all the diesel trucks I had passed on my route. My brakes had gone to the floor with no resistance and giving the message I was now in a direct situation where I had absolutely no control. I became merely a passenger placed at the mercy of where the car was obsessively driving me. This was a direct and forceful pathway into the darkness of the unknown challenging me to bravely face my fate.

The accident about to happen was asking me to give up fighting. I had no option but to yield because I had absolutely no control over the present or future. Emotionally, I immediately became done with fighting to make things right. I had invested so much time and energy for nothing and like that it was all over. I accepted to cut my losses in the few seconds before my wreck terminated, and the chronic stress that gripped me for a long time released from my body. I felt the comfort of calmness as I told myself it was going to be all right, and most of all, I sincerely believed it was true.

Spiritually, it felt like I was not alone, but I really was because I had no passengers. Conceding at a time when I had only known fight became like a blanket of warmth that covered me in safety. It was not a false feeling; it was a divine intervention that had been waiting to rescue me. Trust had become unlocked through my disarmament for the first time since the assault.

Gently, I placed my arms across my chest as if to tuck myself in and felt my body as real. This position made me oddly smile as I thought to myself, "This is how they lay you in a coffin." It wasn't a sinister moment because I had no fear that I would die. I felt so safe waiting for the end because something better for me was approaching.

My car flew off into a culvert and flipped over several times until its final resting place upside down near a tree. The wind had been knocked out of me from the force of flipping, and I was left gasping for air trapped tightly by my seat belt. Dangling upside down was not only something I had never encountered before but it placed me in a serious moment of decision-making. I had to choose between saving myself or hoping someone else would.

I did not want to suffocate and go out that way. I wanted to live. I have the power to change this outcome and felt I had things to do even though I didn't know what they were. I had hit my head hard on the driver's side window until the airbag deployed to protect me. I guess the jarring made the sadness fly out, and for the first time in a long time, I felt in charge because all the noise in my head finally stopped.

Assessing my injuries, I didn't feel anything physically broken but knew it would take a lot of strength to undo my seat belt. It was locked tight with so much force and pressure from holding me in place. I knew I had only one chance for an extreme inhale of breath to release some pressure, but how do I do it while at the same time fighting for air. I was determined to use my only free pass to get it right and release the binding that was holding me prisoner.

It took both hands to have enough strength to unlock the seat belt and finally it worked. I was abruptly slammed to the floor, which was really the ceiling of the car, and thrown into the dashboard. My final resting place had me lying on the inside roof of my car, which was weird, and disorienting because of the inverted angle. Nothing looked familiar not even where the radio was to turn it down. After pulling different levers and buttons in the darkness, I found the door handle and tried to get out, but it would not open because the culvert had bound it shut.

There was filtered darkness inside the car, and the headlights were smashed up against the bank. Lying in broken glass waiting for rescue gave me time to reflect that I had lost my car. I was mad at myself for not being more careful on my late-night drive home. I wanted to cry but could not muster any tears nor did I deserve to have that opportunity, and quite frankly, I was sick of crying.

Loss had become so familiar and ordinary for me by now as I thought of my career, my house, my income, my spirit, and now my car. I had been blaming others for my desperate situation, and here it was smacking me in the face. I had looked inward at this moment and truly found myself responsible for losing my last material possession. Not the predator, not his thugs, not my witnesses, not the superintendent, but me and only me was the one who controlled this outcome.

The trance I had been under had cracked and shown a sliver of light towards life. I was at the bottom of my existence with nowhere to go but up. I had thought I was alone in this horrible journey, but I wasn't. I was just too bullheaded to see that God had another purpose for me and in my sorrow, I had blocked every direction He was trying to lead me. The message was clear I just needed to trust Him.

There was a time when I was willing to give up my life because it seemed the only solution. I had grown to only existing and felt I didn't deserve living. I had accepted loneliness over being surrounded by people. I became the inanimate object the predator had wanted me to believe.

Why would I give up so much to such an unworthy person? The opportunity to breathe life back into my existence is here and now in this exact moment of time if I want to rescue myself.

As I lay in my car, I felt so unnaturally safe and took in the peaceful moment of my vehicle actually protecting me. Maren Morris's song *My Church* was blaring on my awesome sound system. Here I just went through the scariest moment of my life and the song was absolutely beautiful and brought a spiritual peace that could not be explained. I did not want to leave as I lay there in glass, darkness, and alone listening to every lyric and feeling the beat of the sound. This moment made me so strangely clearheaded, and the spirituality of the moment wholly translated into my body and soul as I felt the power of forgiveness would be the catalyst for change.

This path would be a painful process that could not occur overnight. It would be a multitude of factors where my life's experiences, perceptions, and reconciling had to meet center stage. I had to have the strength to see from a different perspective if I wanted to forgive. This meant placing myself in the ungodly shoes of those who violated me. It was going to be an uncomfortable vile world to enter, but the exploration was the only way I would yield freedom.

I had to enter this temporary world in order to create a profound paradigm shift in my life so I could move to a positive direction. I started with empathy for the predator and his team because actually empathizing was who I was unconditionally, so it brought me back to me. Although I hesitated to enter this world, the uncuffing made me alive again where I found purpose and hope had been waiting for my return.

The journey did not mean the predator and his team of violators had to be my friend but wasting time trying to get evil to see light or justice has kept me in an unlived life. I wanted out of that miserable existence, so he, them, and all the others connected to his plan must drift from my thoughts with no opening to return. That is easier said than done when my story has not been validated, so I had to accept it too will be substantiated when I am not a witness.

The continuum of grief, depression, and self-loathing had to be cauterized so it could never seep back and take control of my life. I wanted to align with a new day and finally understood life's valuable tools had not been used because of my despair. They had been waiting for me to pick up so I could build a new different future that was more extraordinary than what I thought I had lost.

I had been wrong in expecting others to mourn my grief and accept my pain. Their journey in our relationship had not experienced the same torture and conflict as mine. I had falsely believed we were enmeshed in understanding each other because in the past, we always had commonality.

This trauma was so different because it was driven on hatred towards my existence, so how could I explain that assault to others? It would be impossible because the people who are in my circle thankfully have not been forced to deal with pathology at such a destructive level.

It took an intense divine encounter to understand I was alone physically but had a purpose that would lead me away from yearning acceptance of my story. I finally acknowledged there needed a disconnect, and it was powerful because now I would be in charge of my direction instead of strapped by the restrictive bindings of seeking validation from a past trauma.

It is not easy for me to say this but I do wish the best for the perpetrators in my school and hope one day they will come to know, surrender, and forgive those who took part in altering their personality towards maleficence.

They too have known an unlived life from childhood because those who had opportunity to protect their innocence ignored the call to action. I wonder what kind of adults they would have come to be if predatory behavior wasn't inflicted on them at such a young age or if they had been given opportunity to experience a safe place to share their traumatic story and effectively process its meaning.

Forgiveness gave me back my power and restored what I thought had been lost forever. New dreams, exploration, and the pursuit of happiness is paving the way for an enriched life, and I'm so in love with the peaceful lifestyle I have created for myself. I have come to believe that "why me" should absolutely be replaced with "why not me!" This is how one achieves full internal freedom to pursue endless dreams and opportunities. There is no way any predator can take this win away from me!

CHAPTER 33:
SCOUT'S BLUEPRINT FOR RECOVERY

ACCEPT

✓   I was a TARGET of hatred NOT A VICTIM.

✓   I need to journal my story instead of seeking validation from others.

✓   Past traumatic events can be triggered. Don't carry old burdens.

✓   Loved ones DO care but have difficulty understanding my story.

✓   Respect yourself even when others do not show compassion.

STOP

✓   Don't get stuck on finding "purpose." Place on hold with "hope."

✓   Don't give away important items.

✓   Declutter living space and donate items I will never use.

✓   Only buy what I need. Don't waste.

✓   Conquer thoughts of self-harm. Accept the future as "unknown."

DISCOVER

✓   Find spirituality. Surrender to where it leads you.

✓   Learn healthy cooking. Buy quality foods. Reduce wasting food.

✓   Make exercise or movement breaks a daily routine.

✓   Notice the beauty in nature.

✓   Forgiveness is key to freedom from people who cause harm.

PROTECTIVE MEASURES

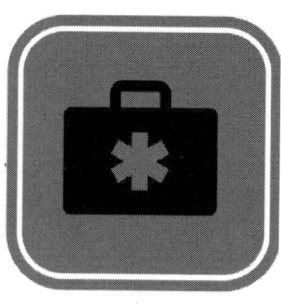

✓   Temporarily suspend social media

✓   Narrow social circle to those who give positive emotional pleasure.

✓   Identify financial burdens and formulate a plan to reduce expenses.

✓   Depression is a time-out. Set a reasonable daily goal.

✓   Find my voice and communicate needs effectively.

BEHAVIOR

✓   Be a better citizen and speak positive language in conversations.

✓   Increase social responsibility i.e., recycling, volunteering etc...

✓   Share talent and skills with others.

✓   Take a journey with someone/pet and make them center of attention.

✓   Seek professional help.